Unflappable

Soaring Beyond a Diagnosis

Jonathan A. Hutton

UNFLAPPABLE PRESS
1910 4th Ave E
PMB 97
Olympia, WA 98506

Certain names and identifying details have been changed.

Cover design by Karolina Wudniak

First paperback edition September 2025

Library of Congress Control Number: 2025918432

ISBN 979-8-9998548-0-3
ISBN 979-8-9998548-1-0 (ebook)

Contents

Introduction

Let's linger on something for a moment, call it a thought experiment if you like. Think back, in time and experience, through all the years you've been alive, and center yourself on a moment or an event, one that's seared into your memory, ever-present. Maybe just recollecting it is uncomfortable, that's okay, stay with it. Perhaps you're thinking about a physical challenge—an illness you endured or witnessed, an injury, a disability. Or maybe the struggle was more ephemeral—a conflict, the loss of a relationship, an emotional wound that lingered, a crippling insecurity. Is it in your mind now, front and center? Now, consider what living through it has taught you. What did you learn from the experience? What are you still learning? I believe that suffering and hardship, unavoidable as they are, can teach us about ourselves, the sort of people we want to be, our priorities in life. The book before you is about the idea of peering into life-altering pains and difficult moments and finding a truth, maybe one that wasn't known to you before.

It's also about paragliding.

When you really get to know someone, over the course of many years, their eccentricities and hang-ups will inevitably bubble to the surface. Here's one of mine: certain idioms and phrases, identifiers and labels that are commonly used in our culture, just rub me the wrong way. Like "cancer survivor." Yes, I'm aware that it's on the back cover of this book. It's shorthand, two words that capture and describe events we're all broadly familiar with; many of us will experience the cancer part one day, although not all will survive it. For some people, this term becomes an important part of their identity, which is another theme throughout this story —what does it mean to be given an identity, one you had no choice in? And how important is it to adopt a new one?

I can tell you're eager to hear more about the flying stuff, which—importantly—is not parasailing. Paragliding is a sport you will learn a lot about in this story. A few things you should know: I am not an expert. I'm still a relatively new pilot, someone who has spent far more time writing than flying, so please do not consider this narrative as advice on how to fly. Flying any sort of small aircraft is dangerous, so do not attempt it without proper instruction. With that said, I encourage everyone I meet to try it by taking a tandem flight with a qualified instructor. Paragliding, and the community of people around it, have become an important part of my life and I hope some of that magic shines through in the story.

Back to words and labels that I have a hard time with— *inspiring*, specifically when used to describe this author. There are plenty of people in the world who gladly affix this label to their real or online personas, many of them have workshops or downloadable content you can buy. I am skeptical, which in turn gives me pause about making any such claim for myself. Perhaps my grift detector is too sensitive, I'm not sure. I wish there was a better word, because *inspiring* feels so fraught. This is another theme you will encounter: sorting through the differences between your conception of self and how other people see you, learning from other perspectives by shifting yours.

A few other things you should know: this is a memoir, a work of non-fiction about real events that occurred in my life over the course of sixteen-plus years, and they are recalled through the lens of my experience and memory. Where possible, I have fact-checked, interviewed, researched and confirmed, ensuring the story is accurate and truthful. Some names have been changed, but most of them have not. Writing this book—like my journey with cancer and my dream of paragliding—has altered my life in beautiful ways I never would have expected and I am so thrilled you are here now, reading it.

Looking for Home

I moved west because I needed distance between my future and a self I wanted to leave behind. At twenty-four, I wasn't directionless, not exactly. West was a direction, and it had a destination: Olympia, Washington. I left Upstate New York, and Georgia too, and started over again.

I had plenty of practice, moving. Every two to three years, our family had a new house in a new state. I grew up with continuous change and novelty—new towns, new friends, new churches. We were a conservative Christian family, but denomination was elastic and flexible. We sampled affiliations like ice cream flavors. Episcopal, Baptist, Methodist, Presbyterian, Nazarene, Apostolic, non-denominational. We attended churches in arenas and basements, strip malls and repurposed gyms. There was always singing, which I liked more than sitting still. There were bands and choirs, hymns and holy pop songs. Sermons might be low-key and earnest or hand-waving performances. The people speaking in tongues and passing out baffled me, but at least it was amusing.

Church and belief was the anchor point for our nomadic army family. It was a home of sorts, an ideological home that was also the unifying concept and the baseline expectation in our large family. Our parents reminded us of this, in no uncertain terms. "All we want is for you to grow up to be Godly adults." I nodded, not knowing how to disagree. I wanted them to be proud, to accept me, but in the end I needed to find my own way—to decide what I wanted, what I believed, who I wanted to be.

I was a precocious and talkative child and then an obstinate teen, but my belief didn't begin to fray until college. At homeschool, there were no guidance counselors, so I chose the University of Least Resistance, one that was far enough away, but in a town with relatives from my dad's side of the family. My parents met there in the early '70s, and my grandparents had been professors. I didn't bother applying anywhere else.

Four years at this university cured me of Christianity. I'd seen and heard enough to know that I believed differently. I looked for opportunities to put distance between myself and the school, along with its belief system, which was a literal pre-requisite. During junior year, I spent a semester out west, in Oregon, reading books, writing papers, and being outside. The US Army had taken us through the Southeast, Midwest, and Southwest, and to near the Rocky Mountains in Colorado. College was in the Northeast, where my parents were from. But the Northwest—with the Pacific Ocean and vast evergreen forests—was where I would go, somewhere far away and new. I could put so many states between me and that school and my family and no one would know the old me. I could become someone else, and find out what I believed.

Growing up in a large family, we learned to not complain, to make do with what we had. As the oldest, I was a caretaker and my needs were secondary to the younger children and the family unit as a whole. I avoided asking for help because I was expected to focus on helping others. I liked—loved—the role of helper. Being the person who assisted others and fixed things would become part of my identity. I was a problem solver, solutions-oriented, take-action sort of person. My youthful years created a sort of scrappy independence. Coupled with my strong will, it's no surprise I set out on my own, westward. I was always going to leave and do things my way, even if I didn't have a plan.

I had helped enough. Years upon years in service to a project that I hadn't chosen, built upon an ideology that wasn't mine. What, exactly, did belong to me? What did I want? What did I believe, independent of the familiar stories, the ones my parents told, the ones they'd heard since childhood? I wanted to find out, so I left.

I arrived in Olympia in 2009, during the Great Recession, and moved into a house full of people. Most of what I owned fit in a suitcase. Our yellow house was near the end of a through street that changed names, for no apparent reason—Walnut and then, inexplicably, 14th.

I met Lindsay briefly on a summer evening. She was a friend of my roommate Nick, and I was floating around in shorts, bare feet on tile floor. She was shy, but clearly amused at the sight of me. I'd stopped taking mood stabilizers and was starting to feel connected to my body again. I didn't mind dancing, shirt off, in front of a stranger. I liked the attention. I was pretty, with shoulder length hair, slender, eyes bright green behind long lashes. I wanted to be unashamed.

In my youth I didn't know what being gay was beyond the fact that you didn't want to be called 'gay.' Ever. And yet, I had met a handful of gay and lesbian Army officers, my dad's superiors. Back in the days of 'don't-ask-don't-tell' the words 'gay' and 'lesbian' were not used, but somehow I knew, and it never struck me as odd or wrong that the colonel my dad worked for lived with another man.

And now I was living in a house with two gay men, Nick and Chad, learning new words to describe ways of being human, identifiers I'd never heard before: gender-fluid, genderqueer, pansexual, transmasculine, non-binary. I admired these people who were so certain about who they were. I still didn't know what category I belonged in.

I did know I liked make up and wearing dresses every now and again, putting on a female persona. It was playful and fun. I'd experimented with it during my years in New York, donning dresses and heels, wearing wigs, introducing myself as Betsy. I loved the attention. I reveled in it. But shame would always find me. There would always be some reminder that my way of being, of looking wasn't quite right. I told myself stories of shame, ones I'd crafted or adapted from words of others. My wrists? Too dainty. My neck? Too long. My arms? Too slender. My voice? Too high. I wanted to be free and bold and open like my friends in Olympia. I wanted to be accepted, but also noticed, desired. I wanted to be needed.

My early experiences with love and dating were met with suspicion and alarm. My relationship with Amanda, my first girlfriend in high school, sent my mother into a fit. She saw us once, parked in the driveway, exchanging kisses.

She sobbed and decried this girl who was stealing her son's innocence. The inversion of the usual gender dynamics were lost on me then, but I got the message. My mom was upset that, as a sixteen-year-old, I was dating girls. I was confused but undeterred, compelled by desire that could not be ignored or wished away.

My parents had their ups and downs but the stability of their marriage was never in question. And in fact, it couldn't be. Divorce, like youthful lust, was a sin, plain and simple. The people who wound up divorced didn't have enough faith. They didn't work hard enough. They didn't have enough strength or wisdom. They failed. And what a shame. Marriage was a holy thing, a sacrament, and everything important was tied up in it—love, romance, sex, babies, major life decisions. Marriage was the foundation upon which you built your life. My parents never bothered explaining *how* you got from dating to the whole marriage part, but youth group and bestselling Christian self-help gurus had plenty of advice, which was mostly "Don't have sex."

The biological realities of being a teenager were never discussed. I only knew bits and pieces because science was generally viewed with skepticism, especially fields that were at odds with a literal interpretation of scripture. We were young earth creationists for a long while—the Christian equivalent of believing the world is flat. Later, I spent years in self-study filling in knowledge gaps from the sanitized homeschool curriculum. But back then, as an effeminate and hormonal teenager, I didn't know anything about my body or how it was changing. My dad would occasionally mention that my judgment was poor because my brain was still growing, which felt like an insult.

All I knew was that I liked talking to and sometimes kissing girls, and that we communicated on a level that was world's apart from how I interacted with boys. Something about the female experience resonated with me, something I never quite understood, and I was learning whatever that harmonic frequency was, it made me attractive to certain girls, the ones who liked my soft features, my long hair, and my smooth skin. I was uncomfortable with these elements of my appearance, but I liked girls, and I loved the attention.

Early on at the yellow house I was working part-time at a bike shop and a shoe store. I had enough money to pay rent. I started hearing about a call center that offered more hours and a better wage and decided to trade my free time for more cash. I applied and got hired (they hired everyone) then made it through training, which weeded out the unserious folks. I'd spent four years at college and very nearly earned a degree in business. Back then, I wanted to be in finance, to out-earn my parents, to accumulate respect by having money. I was shedding Christianity while steeping myself in capitalism. But those ambitions had fallen flat. I interned with a big bank and took a job there after college. I learned quickly that I was completely miserable. The identity I tried to construct came apart—my plans for a career, the belief system I'd discarded, an ill-fated marriage. All of it had failed. I had failed. I was responsible for all of it, not the recession, not my family—me.

And so I found myself at the call center forty or more hours a week. I was good at talking to people, I could type fast and I liked solving problems. I had given up on the idea that I could have a career, that I deserved one, because I'd blown the opportunity. Maybe it was better to just accept that and move on.

"Thank you for calling Horizon Wireless, my name is Jonathan, can I have your first and last name please?"

The greetings were pre-recorded and I listened to the sound of my own voice every time a new call came in. I wasn't proud because basically anyone could do this. There was no prestige in answering phone calls, in being a customer service agent. But I didn't need prestige, I needed a job with paycheck.

Skydiving

My roommate Chad was persuasive, a talker and a keen salesman. It was his idea to go skydiving. I'd been at the call center for two years and although the price was steep—roughly equivalent to a month's rent—I was frugal and had more money than before, so why not?

We arrived at the DZ, or drop zone, which is the place where everyone gathers to train, repack parachutes, and drink beers. And also, to land. We eagerly paid for our tandem jumps and started getting suited up. We were given front-zip jumpsuits and soft padded helmets as the GoPro rolled, capturing us in our pre-flight state. The jump plane was a turboprop with a rolltop door on the side, purpose-built for skydiving, enough space to hold a dozen people or more. The engine started, and a whirring roar filled the runway. Our instructors motioned to us and we climbed into the plane, sitting with our backs to their chests, legs outstretched. The plane accelerated and then we were flying, then climbing. No one could hear anything over the sound of the propellers. The air thinned and I could see my breath. At around 12,000 feet the plane leveled out and slowed.

A few solo jumpers prepare to exit, including a guy in a purple jumpsuit. They fall out of view almost instantly. My senses are overloaded and my mouth is dry. Chad and his instructor are tethered and they slide on their asses towards the open door. I watch as they tumble through the sky. We're next. We slide forward. We are sitting, and my legs are so close to the edge. My instructor checks in, looking at me. I give a thumbs up and we are falling. It's louder than I imagined, like a hairdryer next to my ear, a deafening tunnel of air. My face is rippling, the pressure against my body is immense.

I can only feel the weight of the air. Any sense of falling at 120 mph does not register—everything is blue sky. I trust my instructor, my body and my life are connected to his. I know that I am safe but I cannot make sense of all that's happening and begin to enter a slow-motion state of awareness where I lose track of time and space and left and right. I am thinking nothing. I am feeling everything.

The instructor grabs my hands and pulls them away from my body, out into the open air we're falling through. He invites me to play, to dance with my hands, to feel the speed of our descent. He keeps glancing at his wrist—the altimeter. I feel a tap on my shoulder, a reminder to bring my arms back in, close to my chest. The pilot chute is away and in an instant we are upright, no longer falling but gliding, sailing under canopy.

I can hear again. We are still descending but also moving forward through the air—flying. He puts the controls in my hands and I steer us right and then left. I had no idea parachutes were maneuverable! We set up for landing and I can see Chad and several people. We aren't moving very fast over the ground as my instructor pulls down hard on the controls. I try to stand up as my feet cast a shadow, but the wind catches the parachute and tosses us backwards. I land on my instructor's chest and hear him gasp. Several people run towards us and grab me by the harness. I'm laughing. I apologize for landing on him. There are high fives and hugs and Chad is beaming, with a knowing grin. "We are going to do this again!"

The first skydive is a case study in sensory overload. Everything is new, unpredictable, terrifying and thrilling. We had to skydive again to really appreciate what we'd just done. One tandem, a bucket list item for most, simply wouldn't be enough. We needed to be in the sky, to fall and then save our lives once more. Chad's enthusiasm was hard to ignore, and he convinced me. We would enroll in a training program and become licensed skydivers.

The excitement was so big that neither of us did the math on what it would cost. We wanted skydiving to be more than just a one weekend experience. We understood something about why people do this, jump out of airplanes, fly parachutes. All of the folks at the DZ and on the plane had this calm about them, like they'd learned something about the universe we weren't privy to, not yet anyways. We could be like them—jump and fall and fly like experts, body relaxed, nerves in check. All we needed to do was show up and learn.

Weeks went by and we handled hundreds of calls before we were on a jump plan again, with parachute rigs strapped to our backs. I questioned why I had agreed to this as we prepared for our first training jump, donning harnesses and helmets after finishing half a day of ground training. My palms were wet and my mouth was dry and my head was dazed and pulsing. I felt hungover. I knew what to do in theory—we'd practiced the exit sequence in a replica fuselage and rolled around on the floor on the wheeled things mechanics use under cars, except on our stomachs, simulating proper belly to earth position. *The nerves will settle once I just do this*, I thought. *I can do this. I can jump out of this plane and throw my main at the right time.*

The air feels even colder than before as we approach altitude. We slow, the engines calm from a roar to a hum, and the door rolls up—*whooooosh*, like a wave crashing. Chad goes first. I watch him but I'm concentrating on what I need to do, what I practiced. I'm standing, semi-crouched, hand tightly gripping a bar on the inside of the plane. One instructor is halfway outside the door already, the other on my right side. We look at each other, checking in. I give the signal, still nervous but committed. We exit the plane in a single motion, as a unit. We are falling together towards the earth at 120 mph. There is only the sound of air rushing by. My instructors are holding me on either side, each one with a hand on my forearm and hip. I look at my altimeter. I reach behind to touch my pilot chute. Just like we practiced, right arm, reaching down and behind to my right hip. *It's still there. Good.* I bring my right arm back to where it was, above my head, like I'm in one of those body scanners at the airport.

Altimeter check—8,000 feet. We're getting closer. Seconds are like minutes because I am only focused on this task. One more practice touch. 5,500 feet. I wave my arms above my head like a referee and my instructors acknowledge they are ready to fall away. I reach behind again, this time grabbing ahold of the pilot chute's ball and throwing it away from my body. There's a brief moment, a second or two, where I'm still flat, belly to earth, as the pilot opens the main. I go from falling at terminal velocity to a more pleasant speed. I look up and my canopy is there, just as it should be.

I scream out in joy and relief. I am under a canopy, no longer falling, flying on a parachute which is descending but also moving forward. I can see so much of Mason County, 4,000 feet above the ground. The canopy is holding me, I am suspended in open space, in the same air birds travel in, flying. I am secure here above and away from all those earthly concerns.

The parachute was open and I wasn't falling. I was suspended in the air, held by a canopy above, secure in my harness. There was no space in my mind for anything besides the present moment and forward motion, the gravity and air, the sound of wind whipping past my face. I could see treetops and building, the city to the west, the DZ and airport, half a mile down below my feet. I wasn't afraid or ashamed, there was no such thing as failure. I was here in the sky, flying. I did not want to land but this is the purpose of a parachute, to catch you, to stop the fall and bring you back to the ground. The time sailing through the air was short lived, but I knew I wanted more.

Chad and I did a few more training jumps before we ran out of money. Our call center wages could not support a skydiving habit. If I'd had a better job, maybe I would've continued, but I began to realize what I really wanted was to fly the canopy. The jumping and falling part was so brief, chaotic and loud. It was an adrenaline jolt, sure, but flying the parachute around, above the DZ, was serene and magical. I wanted more of that, more flying, without the falling and the deafening noise. I thought about asking the instructors if it was possible to just fly a parachute, but it seemed like a foolish question, an affront to their sport. So, I googled it at home. I probably typed something like *can you fly a parachute without skydiving?* Almost immediately, I found the answer. Yes, you can, and it's called paragliding.

I found videos of pilots soaring from mountains, over valleys and rivers, covering great distances. One launched from Mount Fuji, flying through cloud, landing miles away. I was mesmerized by the calmness and the vistas they must have seen. They were flying under this thing that resembled a parachute, but bigger, wider and shaped more like an arc. And there was no throwing, no falling—the wing appeared overhead at the pilot's command and then in a moment, he leaves the ground. The steps looked balletic, effortless. I could imagine that feeling, seeing those pilots flying their wings, being held by the air, moving through it with such ease. I had experienced something like that with the parachute, but this was a different form of flight that seemed more tranquil and quiet. I knew I needed to do this. I was utterly convinced—I would learn how to fly a paraglider.

The dream was as big as my undergrad aspirations, when all I wanted was a career in high finance. But flying was something else, I was certain I could do it and I didn't need a degree or an internship. I started researching and checked out a copy of *The Art of Paragliding* by Dennis Pagan from the library. I began having dreams about flying, soaring through the air. I continued to marvel at the fact this even existed, this form of flight that appeared to be so perfect. I wanted to be in the air again, feel what I had under that canopy after falling from the plane. I didn't know how or when but I was certain that one day I would fly a wing like the ones in the videos. I would soar and leave the earth for a while, saying goodbye to all the stress and mundane things, and simply be in the sky.

There was a new freedom, being up there, flying. When you are a few thousand feet above the earth, something changes, not for everyone but for those who can revel in it, who continue to want more. My mind was free, open to the earth around me, when I was in the sky. I didn't care about anything else—I couldn't. It simply wasn't possible because all of that space was consumed by the air surrounding and holding me. There were no jobs, no money, no expectations or disappointments, no shame. I was free of those things, and from myself too.

My assumption was that paragliding would cost as much, or more, than skydiving. A few thousand for training, a few thousand more for all the gear. I didn't have that sort of money, nor did I have the flexibility to take time off work when I wanted. If I was going to learn how to fly, I would need a new job, a career. But first, I would need to find a new place to live.

Westside to East

The yellow house experiment was predicated on trust. Trust that rent would be paid once collected, usually in cash, from our roster of roommates. In turn, the rental company would leave us be, and provided we didn't upset any neighbors, we could carry on. The rent got skimmed and we pissed off the wrong parents on the other side of the fence. After too many late payments and noise complaints, we had to move.

In the early 2010s, affordable rentals were easy to come by in Olympia, so it didn't take long to find a new house. The duplex on Puget St was where we found ourselves, most of us anyways. Brandon, Beau, and April were on one side, with me, Casey, Zac on the other. Chad and Nick had broken up and gone their separate ways. I was thankful to be living with people I knew, and still working at the call center. It was a job with an hourly wage that was a clock-bound game where you resolved issues in a fixed window of time. You were judged on the averages. It required speed, precision, attention to detail, and some measure of charm.

After a while, I was a pro. I could handle any inquiry, I was knowledgeable, resourceful, my survey scores were high.

The supervisors noticed and I started coaching other agents, allowing them to shadow me, or helping in real time doing floor support. This was the pathway to a promotion. Two years in, I became a manager and had a team of my own. The work was not glamorous and I was expected to give significantly more time and effort for marginally more pay, but the allure of this accomplishment, the prestige of being a leader was enough. For a while, anyways.

I started dating a woman named Andrea. We'd first met when I was still an agent. She was funny and bold and beautiful in her self-confidence. I fell hard, and was unable to do much beyond working and being in love, planning out a future together that I would nurture into existence. I would've done anything for Andrea then. Almost anything. I wasn't going to move to California. And so she left and I cried and biked and worked, and for a while, I forgot about flying.

Eventually, I tired of the supervisor role, the long hours and endless conflicts with customers, the cycles of hiring and firing. I was approaching four years in a warehouse of cubicles and even though I'd been promoted, the workload was not aligned with the pay. Worse, I was getting bored. This was a problem because when I get bored I go looking for new things to fix, new projects to take on. Plenty of things were broken at the call center, some intentionally, all of them above my pay grade. I knew I needed to leave when I realized there was nothing new for me to do, nothing the company wanted from me besides more of the same. Hire, train, coach, fire, take calls. Over and over again. I had so much more to give.

I needed to prove myself somewhere else because the call center was a dead end. So I went looking for a role where I could put my skill to better use, where I would be valued. I found an ad for a Customer Service Manager position at an internet retailer. I was qualified, confident that I could excel, because I had before. Finally, I would be doing something new.

The interview was at the company's headquarters, in an office building outside of town near the airport. I was ready for a challenge. I explained my background and skills with managing a team. I met the owner and his daughter, who ran the marketing department. They offered me the job and I left the call center. Finally, I was making progress.

The internet company paid me more than the call center, closer to what I imagined I deserved, which wasn't much. I didn't really need much. The duplex was cheap, and we split the rent three or four ways, depending on how many roommates we had at any given time. And I didn't own a car. I commuted on my bike, like I'd done for years. I was so proud that I'd moved on from the call center after four years; this was the big step I'd needed to take and I'd been preparing without even knowing it. I was ready to put all my energy into this job, hopeful that it would become something more than a job in time. I just needed to prove myself.

I worked more hours than before. I attended conferences, I researched new vendors and technology platforms. I built things—processes, workflow, whole systems. I coached and managed and met with the top bosses. I walked around with a swagger I'd never had before. "I run the customer service operations for an internet retailer," I explained, when people asked me what I did for a living. I was proud of where I was, what I'd managed to accomplish. I was a career person now.

My bike rides to the office were invigorating, and I'd arrive energized and ready to deliver, to contribute. The summer dissolved into another damp and mossy fall. I biked harder, rain or shine, and worked even more. I didn't take time off because what would that say about my work ethic? As the new manager, it was understood that I would work more hours than the people on my team.

I'd started taking the little white pills when spring allergens peppered the air. It was March, the ground was still damp but the skies were clear blue, and my thirtieth birthday was weeks away. I'd rolled into work and followed the usual routine, changing out of my cycling clothes into my business casual outfit.

The CEO wanted to meet with me first thing, which was odd. We sat in the second floor conference room and he explained that we needed to let go of two people on my team, they were no longer a good fit at the company. His daughter sat next to him, nodding in agreement. I was confused by the timing. Why today? I was aware one of my agents was already in the crosshairs. The owner did not like her—she was too liberal, too much of a hippy type, she had "an attitude." She was good at her job, but that didn't matter. She needed to go.

I'd fired many people in my time at the call center, and after a while I was numb to it. The internet company had a stable staff, with low turnover, which had been part of the appeal. I didn't love firing people, but I did it and watched as their faces fell. I felt sympathy for them, but in a detached, *just doing my job* sort of way.

Another meeting was scheduled, presumably to follow up on the terminations. The owner set a piece of paper on the conference room table and slid it towards me. I recognized the company letterhead. I was fired too.

My Plans Go South

Panic set in quickly. I was making progress towards a career and now that was gone. I was reliving the failed experiment with banking. I'd given this company so much of myself without any thought. I trusted them to take care of me because they said we were family. And I fell for it. I hadn't been skeptical enough because I was eager, inexperienced. I couldn't think about flying while my life was imploding. I hadn't been fired before; I was the one who did the firing.

I could feel fragments of my identity coming apart, the stories I'd been telling myself were myths, useful fictions, about a future with this company, one where I'd be a senior manager, then maybe an executive. I had become so invested in the idea of a career in this company, that I hadn't considered what I might do if it didn't work out. I didn't have a plan B because I barely had a plan A. I knew I needed to leave the call center, that I deserved more, that I was capable, smart. And I took the first thing that I found, I jumped without hesitation, without looking first. And my instinct was wrong, my trust misplaced. The work I did was rewarded with a hostile goodbye.

At the call center we had a community. We all needed to pay the bills, which is why we were there. Our employer was exacting and we were little more than lines on a bar graph, but we knew that. The notion of an outsourcing company being a family would've been cause for laughter and mockery. Everyone knew the score. We were there because we had to be and we made friends and celebrated each other, at work and out in the real world, away from the rows of cubicles. I wanted something similar to that at the internet company, it seemed reasonable. But I was naive, I couldn't or didn't want to see that I was just as expendable as at the call center. My employers were not friends, we didn't have a community—that was just a facade, something I let myself believe because it was easier to justify the hours, the personal sacrifices.

I had worked my way into believing that my value as a person, my identity, was inseparable from work. The belief was so powerful that it didn't even register as belief, it was just a fact, not something to interrogate or thoughtfully consider. *I am my work.* This amplified the loss. Not having a job, being unemployed, much less being fired, was the definition of failure. I had a career, a chance, I'd found something I was good at, and then I failed. Catastrophically. *What kind of fool lets this happen? How could I ever recover?* I was worthless without gainful employment.

I hated the quiet, open-ended space of not knowing when and how the next job would materialize. Gaps in employment were shameful, a stain on one's resume. I was so stupid. I didn't see the signs. My boss had recently left, because of the long commute he'd explained, and then the daughter had taken over his role. Of course. Why wasn't I savvier? They were plotting in plain sight and I wasn't the least bit alarmed. I was clueless.

I'd lost my job but at least I had someone who needed me. I'd met Abbi after Andrea, after leaving the call center. She was taller than me, funny, full of charm and wild stories. Her house sat at the end of the same street as the duplex, blocks away. We fought, but not always. Usually it had something to do with me, something I wasn't doing, or was doing too much of.

I was desperate for a new job and after months looking, I found a temporary role. I could breathe again. The temp job resembled the call center—rows of computers and phones, with a simple objective: output. There were no survey scores, no call times, just backlogs of tickets that needed eyes, and sometimes a phone call to a customer. I understood the work and did it well but was cautious. The internet company and the experience of being fired, had me on high alert. I would not make waves. I would keep my head down and work and then maybe eventually I could figure out a new career path. I wasn't sure customer service was where I wanted to be.

The rented office was downtown, which made my bike ride from the duplex laughably short. The internet company was a solid seven-mile jaunt, and now I was less than one mile away from my workplace. I walked some days, or rode the bus down the hill, listening to music on bright white earbuds. I always had tissues on me, stashed in pockets or in my backpack, folded neatly until used, and then crumpled and stuffed into a different pocket. The drip had not stopped. It was a nuisance, but I felt fine and carried on, going to work, to shows, to my favorite beer bar, to Abbi's house.

The runny nose annoyed her and she insisted that I go see someone. I figured an allergist was the logical starting point. I must be allergic to *something*, why else would my nose run day and night? All of the over the counter meds—Allegra, Zyrtec, Benadryl—I'd tried them. Nothing. The drip continued.

The new job—the temp position—was going fine, but my relationship with Abbi was in a pendulum. We were stable, we were taking a break. We were having fun, she was drunk and yelling. She still loves me, she's telling me to move out. We're going to make it work, "why are you so fucking selfish?!" I started spending more time going to shows, taking on side projects. I was working and finding new reasons to put distance between us because the back and forth was too much. If I wasn't a career person, maybe I could be a good partner and a helper, but now that felt uncertain too.

Our fights got worse, especially when she was drinking. I did not know how to ask for help, to make an exit, to give an ultimatum. She always promised to do better, but if I saw something that resembled remorse, it was always couched in a way that placed the responsibility on me.

"Well, if you hadn't said... "

"Of course you know, you should have known that... "

"I wasn't actually going to... "

"You're fine, aren't you?"

She could not own up to misbehavior, no matter how awful. There was always an excuse. But I stayed. I didn't think anyone else could love me like she did, and I had already invested so much of my self into this project. I wasn't thinking about flying because I had become enamored with the idea of being desired and useful to a partner. I was certain that being in a relationship was what I needed then. I had so much to give. I needed to be needed.

It's Not Allergies

I made an appointment with an allergist and rode my bike to the clinic. The nurse gave me a test and I waited in the brightly lit room as red dots formed in neat rows on my left arm. The young, well-groomed doctor returned, examining my arm before speaking:

"Well, it looks like you are allergic to every sort of grass species in the region. We could try something like allergy shots, but honestly you should consider moving."

A wave of anger widened my eyes. *Grass allergies are not the reason. He is dead wrong.* I was outraged that he would prescribe relocation as a solution, it was lazy—where did he study medicine? I took a breath, searching for a response. Outbursts are not my style so I swallowed the rage and smiled in a fake sort of way, the sort of smile you put on when you're trying to make a polite exit from an impossible situation. I needed to leave, to be far away from this hack and his bullshit advice.

There was a cause for this annoyance that required me to carry tissues everywhere I went, we just needed to find it.

For months and months, I'd tried allergy meds and nothing helped. I carried tissues everywhere, stuffed into pockets, but I didn't feel sick or congested. The drip persisted. Summer to winter, indoors and out; it was a nuisance and I wanted it fixed. I knew there were doctors who specialized in noses and ears, but I had never seen one because I could hear just fine and this was the only problem I'd ever had with my nose. In general, I was healthy, which made the runny nose even more vexing. I didn't get colds, I couldn't remember the last time I'd had the flu—probably childhood —and in four years at the call center, I'd taken zero sick days because I was never sick.

I saw an ENT a few weeks after the allergist. Dr. Russell was gray-haired and wore glasses. I explained my runny nose, that I was confident allergies were *not* the issue. I mentioned I'd have nosebleeds occasionally, mostly when I used Afrin. Dr. Russell nodded. "Let's have a look," he said, saddling up to a rolling stool. He examined my nasal cavities, prying them open with a tool that fit inside the contours of my nose. He squinted, looking through little magnifiers set against his glasses. He looked curious, intrigued by what he was seeing.

The CT scanner was just down the hall. The office felt a little like a dentist's—self-contained, unlike a clinic in a big hospital. The technician, a nurse, finished my scan and I was guided back to the exam chair. Dr. Russell looked at the monitor and then at me. He explained there was something, but didn't say what it might be. He wanted to take a sample, a biopsy. The inverse nose pliers came back out. I was wearing a button up, with a work lanyard around my neck. He sprayed a numbing agent and then guided what looked like a pair of tiny scissors deep into my right nostril. I felt the cold metal on the inside of my nose, and pushed myself further back into the chair. The old nose doctor clipped a bit of flesh with his scissors and I winced. Blood started to run, dripping on my bright green lanyard. He hadn't bothered to drape me in his eagerness. Dr. Russell explained that he would send the sample off for testing and then give me a call.

I left Dr. Russell's office with a bloodstained lanyard feeling like we were making progress, that soon I would have an explanation. There was probably some growth up there, a simple thing that could be cut out and then problem solved, like removing a wart. I didn't give the biopsy much thought until the doctor called me to explain his usual lab couldn't identify the sample. *Huh, that's odd.* He explained that it would need to be analyzed at another lab, in Seattle. They would identify it and I'd get a call from him as soon as the results came in. I was a little worried now, confused why my little growth wasn't something they recognized. Maybe the lab wasn't very specialized. Maybe my cells were just a little odd. The words malignancy and cancer had not yet entered my vocabulary.

A week went by and work continued. I was ready to have an answer and the most likely explanation, I reasoned, was probably something simple, so I didn't worry. We were going to solve this problem, and maybe that would mean meds or minor surgery. No big deal. I went back to my temp job. A percentage of the big group originally hired had been let go as the project wound down. I had my own desk now and more responsibility, still working out of a rented office space in downtown, across from the Starbucks.

The day was moving along at an unhurried pace. I opened an email with a new assignment and began looking through a spreadsheet, considering how long this task would take me to complete. I reviewed a few examples, taking note of patterns. Another email notification popped up on screen—an urgent request. I switched tasks and started typing out a response. I hadn't glanced at my phone in a while so I pulled it from my pocket. *Shit. Dr. Russell's office.* He'd left a voicemail:

"Hello, Mr. Hutton... wanted to let you know we've received the lab results back and I was hoping to discuss them with you. Can you give me a call back at your earliest convenience?"

Why didn't he just explain the results in his message?

I dialed the number and waited on hold as my eyes darted around, looking for something to fix on, a solid object, words on a contact list taped to the wall, the fire extinguisher sign. In most cancer stories, people recall that moment, when they receive the diagnosis. It's something like the memory of where you were on 9/11. All of the details are there and you can rewind back to when you found out and peer into it.

Dr. Russell spoke and I listened, trying to absorb everything he was saying.

He explained that the pathology showed I had a malignant tumor. I was confused—malignant, as in cancer? In my nose? How is that even possible? I'd never heard of such a thing. What were the odds? No one in my family, no one I'd ever met had *nose* cancer. I hadn't even considered the possibility because it was so far from any part of my experience. My runny nose was caused by a cancerous tumor, which felt absurd, like the punch line in a bad joke. I would be receiving a copy of the lab report, Dr. Russell explained, but I should go ahead and make an appointment now with a specialized ENT in Seattle. He would be referring me to a doctor he knew.

After months of waiting I finally had an answer, an explanation for the runny nose, the nosebleeds, the annoyances that presented like seasonal allergies, except they were all-seasons. I was still at work, but I wouldn't be getting my assignments done today.

It's hard not to go down an internet search rabbit hole when you finally have a name for your problem. I had an acronym too—ITAC. Intestinal type adenocarcinoma. It's called this because under the microscope, the cells resemble a more common cancer that's usually found in the gut. Researchers still do not have a comprehensive understanding of why this and other types of malignancies manifest themselves in the head/neck region, in seemingly random ways. Of the sinonasal cancers, it was rare but not the rarest. The survival stats weren't encouraging—one study cited a 35% mean five-year survival rate, but most of the patients were twenty, thirty, forty years older than me. I read about treatment protocols, pathology, and grading. Before I saw the oncologist, I wanted to be immersed, to learn the language of cancer treatment. I was frantic in my curiosity. Knowing was better than not knowing, so I went looking. I wanted to be prepared, even though I didn't know what to expect.

It was January, barely six months into my new job, and I'd just received a cancer diagnosis. The timing was less than ideal. I wondered what it would be like to become a statistic on one of those charts with mortality rates, to die just as my life and career were beginning to take shape. I imagined my family would not handle this well—they would be alarmed and disoriented once I told them. I was determined to respond differently, to reframe whatever fear I had of the unknown into something else—to try and be calm about the whole cancer thing, because once I started to tell people, they'd begin to freak the fuck out. There was no sense in having a similar reaction, so I resolved not to.

People would ask how and why this happened, what caused my cancer, but as I read more about the disease, I learned that science didn't really have a good answer; the why was unknowable. So I could accept that or be mad about it. Was anger going to help me get through this, if getting through was even possible? I'd carried so much anger and resentment—towards my parents, the church, the religion I hadn't chosen—but how could I be angry at randomness, at misbehaving cells, my cells? I didn't have a choice in the disease, but I did have control over how I navigated it.

I never expected life to be fair or just or equitable, I could only face it with eyes open. I was going to learn everything I could, listen to my doctors, be a good patient. I had no idea what to expect, if this was going to hurt, what my body would feel like after, what the oncologists would say, how my life might change. Maybe the change would simply be an end.

I thought about my family, how they might weather a similar diagnosis, what divine interventions they might call on. I didn't believe in miracles or life after death or god. Even hearing someone say *I'm praying for you* made me bristle because it felt presumptuous, and reminded me of the old person I'd left behind. Knowing someone was praying would not change the outcome. I told my family to keep the prayer talk to themselves. My mother seemed surprised when I said this, when I called to share the news of the diagnosis. "Oh, okay honey, if that's what you want."

I started telling friends in Olympia about my diagnosis and the reactions varied widely—from tearful embraces to righteous anger, "I'm so sorry, this is horrible" to "dude, fuck cancer, you're going to beat this thing." People who've been through cancer know that much of what you hear early on is irrelevant or unhelpful; the shock of learning that someone you know has cancer can be stupefying, which might explain why people blurt out cancer stories ("Oh, wow, yeah my aunt had cancer... she died two years ago") or share questionable remedies ("You know, these mushroom supplements have been shown to destroy cancer cells... I can get you some"). People mean well, but often say some weird shit.

I told my boss, Joanna, not knowing what this would mean for my job. I needed health insurance for treatment and it would be challenging to afford it without being employed. Since I was still new, I had no real protections, no certainty that I would have a job waiting for me after I finished treatment. Joanna understood the situation I was in, and promised me my job would be safe. She spoke like someone who had been through big challenges in life before and I trusted her, intuitively.

My brother Tim, a second year medical student, called and we spoke about the what-ifs—terminal outcomes, advance directives, last wishes. Abbi didn't say much. Our relationship continued to be precarious, but I was hopeful that with enough time and discussion we could work things out; maybe getting through my cancer together would be the way that happened.

Treatment = Seattle

I saw my new ENT just two weeks after the diagnosis, at a big hospital in downtown Seattle. Dr. Bayles was tall with curly blonde hair, he spoke directly, with what sounded like the remnants of a Southern accent, as he explained the surgery to remove the tumor from my face. He was confident he could excise it with good margins, which meant removing healthy tissue around the cancer, hopefully reducing the odds of recurrence. Surgery would come before any potential treatment. Bayles, like Russell, was baffled by the type of malignancy, already rare but basically unheard of in a thirty-year-old.

The oncology floor was modern and sleek, recently remodeled with donor money. Sitting in the waiting room, I see mostly old people, with a few middle-aged folks sprinkled in. No one looked happy to be there. After my vitals, I was ushered into an exam room with a big sliding glass door to wait for my oncologist. Dr. Vishnu greeted me with a warm handshake. I peppered him with questions about the knowns and unknowns of the disease, treatment protocols, grading, mean survival. He was present and engaged, providing thorough answers and caveats about the limits of present day oncology. I was reassured by his steadiness. I asked if he'd ever treated another patient around my age with the same cancer— just one. I had no desire to be special in this way, but now I was an oncological anomaly. *Maybe I'll be in a journal article someday.*

Dr. Vishnu walks me through the recommended course of treatment. After surgery, I'd undergo chemo and radiation concurrently. Patients at a more advanced age probably wouldn't tolerate an aggressive approach like this one, but I'm young, healthy. He assures me I will bounce back. Aggressive treatment would give me the best chance of a curative outcome. This logic makes sense: rare cancer + young age + aggressive treatment = long-term success (hopefully). I trust this man to know what's best even though he doesn't know everything. He can't because I am an outlier. If we were talking about something more common, he would mention research about the efficacy of different treatments, the usual long-term outcomes. There would be a body of knowledge on which to rely, an established set of protocols to follow, and a community of similar patients to connect with.

There's no debrief on the whole rare cancer thing after a diagnosis. You begin to learn that you've entered an area of medicine where art and science meet in a best guess, trial and error sort of way. You become part of the experiment. This nuance is completely lost on most people—for them, there's no meaningful difference between the common and rare cancers; cancer is cancer, you get treatment, and then you beat it and move on with life. The idea that medical professionals—highly trained specialists—might lack certainty about what to do or what might happen is a strange place to find yourself.

Treatment was set to begin a month after surgery—chemo and radiation, five days a week for two months. Monday through Friday, I would need to be in Seattle, but asking for rides was too much to stomach. Getting to treatment would be a project I needed to manage. A friend's mom, a nurse, had offered to drive me, but I couldn't bring myself to ask. I was not supposed to need that much help, cancer or otherwise. I could solve this on my own and the solution seemed clear—I would temporarily move to Seattle. I didn't love the idea of paying rent in two places, but I'd managed to stash away enough savings that I wasn't worried.

I'd researched housing options for cancer patients but I didn't qualify; I lived too close and didn't have children who required care. A friend of mine suggested I reach out to his mom and stepfather, who lived outside of Seattle—they might be able to put me up during treatment. We chatted on the phone and I explained my dilemma. They asked if I was a believer, a Christian, which seemed like an odd screening question. I said I wasn't, but had been raised in the church. "Well, we'll need some time to pray on this... as a family."

I got a voicemail a few days later. They were sorry, but unfortunately, they couldn't help me, it just wouldn't work. They didn't say why, exactly, but I knew. I was not surprised. I scoured Craigslist for short-term rentals and found one that was cheap enough. I emailed and explained my situation. The house was a craftsman next to a Shell station in North Seattle. There were two guys living there, both named Peter. Abbi drove me to Seattle, annoyed I needed her help, that she had to take time off work, that I didn't have a car. I did not want to upset her because I hated those moments, the threats, the cutting words. I thanked her and tried to be less needy.

Treatments were at the hospital downtown, so I'd ride the express bus in the morning and walk up the hill to the medical complex. I'd had a PICC line placed in my arm for the chemo infusions, which is basically a semi-permanent IV with a light purple dongle. I would sit in a medical-grade recliner as the dose of cisplatin was delivered. The IV bags it came in were handled cautiously, marked with bright symbols indicating their toxicity. First the chemo, then saline.

Radiation was in the basement. I'd take the elevator down, guiding a five-wheeled IV bag holder. After a while, I was on a first name basis with all of the nurses and technicians. Each treatment took about thirty minutes—I would lie on my back, on a table near a hulking machine that resembled a CT scanner as the technician secured me in place with a custom face mask made from green plastic mesh. I would be held in place, ensuring precise delivery of radiation to my face and neck.

Often, the techs would ask if I was okay, if I was experiencing claustrophobia. "No, I'm just fine." I didn't mind being here, immobilized for a short while; if I relaxed completely, I could rest. I smiled and thanked the staff when I left. I wasn't in any pain yet, and I had the routine down. On the way back to the gas station house I'd stop and get a chocolate milkshake with whipped cream; my oncologist said I should consume a lot of calories.

I was sure that I could manage treatment, that I could weather the chemo and radiation, that side effects would be minimal and then life would be normal again. Everyone I knew—Abbi, my friends—was in Olympia; I'd be fine on my own for eight weeks. A month in, eating became more difficult. Nothing tasted like food. Everything was bland. Then, just looking at food made me queasy. My mouth started to hurt as sores formed on my tongue and palate. Saline rinses twice a day were supposed to help, but I stopped when the saltwater made me want to vomit.

My ribs were starting to show from all the weight loss. The walk to the bus stop was a fever dream—everything around me was blurry and moving at 2x speed, but I was just standing there, stuck in slow motion. I was too sick to eat or drink. Everything turned to vomit and the meds did nothing. IV fluids were routine and my veins were becoming a challenge. My oncologist decided a stomach tube for liquid nutrition was necessary. I stayed in the hospital overnight and woke up with a six inches of plastic tubing jutting out of my stomach, nearly in the center of my chest. I took an Uber back to the gas station house, tube grazing a t-shirt that no longer fit, loose around my chest and arms.

Reality started to loosen and mirrors became unsettling; the reflection was not someone I knew. Motion and moving were clipped, missing frames, slowing to a pause. I had no thoughts but still managed to keep the schedule. I went to treatment and then into blankness, sleep—but not the restful kind—devoid of dreams, mouth parched and body aching. I wanted to be home but I had no home. Abbi was not home, she was not even a partner. *Why are we still together?* I needed so much more than I had the ability to ask for; asking, needing to ask, was failure. But I *had* tried—Abbi, the family outside Seattle.

I was on my own, too sick to plan, to find a solution, to think. The whole thing was cruel, dark, and lonely. After two months, I was finally done with treatment, but getting even sicker, because of the radiation. I managed to pack up the room in Seattle. Abbi did not have a face, she was a blur of white and blonde. She wore her favorite blue jacket. I was back in Olympia but I was only a sick, beleaguered stack of bones, uncertain how I'd gotten there. I was back at the duplex and she was at her house. She said something—she couldn't deal with me, with this—the words were garbled, but I understood: I was going to be alone.

Recovery was a blank space of several weeks. I wasn't dreaming of flying. I wasn't dreaming at all because the sickness and the drugs erased anything resembling a dream. I could barely recognize the basic elements of the day—time, calendar dates, sunrise, sunset. I was still alive but something less than a functional human being, no longer productive, unable to think or plan, only reacting. I had no memory of being so helpless and infant-like. I didn't anticipate the scale of this sickness.

I'd managed to summon the energy to call my boss and explain that I would need additional time before returning to work. I hadn't planned on being so sick, on needing to recover like this. I could barely talk and the haze of opioids kept my eyes in a half focus. The stomach tube was how food and medicine entered my body; cartons of liquid nutrition sat in the corner of my room, meds were on the dresser. I had just enough strength to feed myself and then I would rest, curled up, alone.

Slowly, I started to feel again, the ache began to subside, there was less bile in my mouth. I tapered down the narcotics and took the fentanyl patch off. I went outside and stood on the sidewalk, tired, amazed my legs could hold me.

I could not live with Abbi anymore. I finally understood there was nothing left to salvage. I needed to leave.

I was eager to eat solid food again, after weeks of feeding myself through a tube. At first, the slightest bit of heat or acid stung every surface in my mouth. I ate cautiously, but started to gain weight. I was no longer in a fog, done with the awful and necessary pain meds. Soon, I was back on my bike, wind in my face, flying down hills.

I went back to work with the tube still in. My doctors insisted that I wait to have it removed, just in case. I was annoyed, but relented; I wasn't going to argue. I could wait another few weeks and then I would be done with this vestige of my suffering. Placing the stomach tube had required surgery and staying overnight in the hospital—the removal took minutes. The hole in my chest closed, leaving a crooked dimple of a scar.

A year went by and there were no more side effects or limitations. I could eat spice and vinegar, I could drink beer. I was still with Abbi because I hadn't yet figured out how to leave. Work was stable and I was approaching two years there, earning a decent salary—more than the call center and the internet company. My frugality hadn't changed though. I was still living a minimum wage lifestyle and saving everything else. At home one weekend, I came across an internet ad: "Check today to see if you qualify!" I clicked out of curiosity. I qualified for a mortgage. *Okay, wow, I think I'm going to buy a house.*

I hadn't planned it, but this would be my way of leaving, of putting distance between us, drawing a line to separate my world and hers and then closing the door. Buying a house. This would be the final act, my way of saying "Goodbye Abbi, I cannot do this anymore." If I was going to leave her, we could not live on the same street; the proximity would be too much. I would be pulled back in. She would want to stay friends and I would say yes because she was sorry and at least I can give her that, right? I did not know myself as well then, but I did know that I needed distance.

I knew I would lose friends. Abbi was charming and fun to be around and so they would choose her. She cultivated a persona that was sympathetic and had answers and reasons to justify every action. Her stories back then framed our troubles very differently, and it's easier to believe the familiar narrative—a manipulative and arrogant man who asked for too much, who took advantage of a woman and then tried to rewrite the story and make himself the victim. I couldn't blame them for believing that version. I wanted to believe it too, earlier, when I was ashamed, when I thought I deserved what was happening.

And I was not faultless. I wanted the relationship to be something it was never meant to be: stable, healthy, supportive. I gave everything I could without pausing to ask why, without knowing the landscape of my own insecurities. I was repeating the same mistakes as before, trying to believe something into existence, like I had with Andrea, with the internet company too. I wanted to be secure and needed and cared for and that would mean giving all of myself, without question. I did not understand slow and measured, boundaries and healthy distance. I was selfish in this want, for everything all at once, and careless in my grasping.

But I did not deserve abuse. No one does. And I thought that I could forgive my way out of those cycles, that the repairs would hold, that me being in therapy and reading books would help change her. I'd been deluded, hopeful in a destructive way, blind to the truth of where I was, what we had. It took being left, during recovery, to understand that. Afterwards, I was biding my time without knowing it, putting more and more space between us, slowly, safely stepping away.

I bought the house and told her it was over. She was confused—"... but *why*?" I explained why, the being left, the abuse. She told me I was full of myself and a liar; it didn't happen, not like that. She had been there for me, who was I to complain? What about all of the things I had done, the ways I failed her? For a while I was angry, and then just sad, mostly for her. I was glad I left, that I had a place, a home away from her. She reached out and asked if we could be friends, if she could text me, if we could stay in touch. Wisely, a friend steadied me when I wasn't sure, when I wanted to change my mind and start talking to her again. I still loved her as a person—a sad, broken person, someone who needed help and care. But I needed to recover, to guard myself.

"No, I can't. I'm sorry."

Lindsay

Lindsay almost didn't respond to my message on the app because my user name had the word *cyclist* in it. Maybe she thought I wouldn't be interested because of her body type or bookishness. I'd always been trim but wasn't judgy or particularly attracted to rail-thin figures. Our conversation began online and quickly moved into the real world.

We first met in the fall, at the bar where I used to do my laundry on the weekends, back when I lived at the run-down duplex. She wore a big smile with a pair of slightly crooked front teeth, one overlapping the other. I'd noticed her shared photos were mostly close mouthed, perhaps she was embarrassed, self-conscious. Her round face and gray streaks were adorable and her laugh was rosy and warm, like her voice.

I'd been so distracted, searching for who I was and what I wanted, but now I was at my favorite bar, with this lovely woman. I told her about my cancer and recovery, the new house. She talked about her best friends, the farm where she'd grown up, the road named after her family. We were meeting for the first time, we thought, but soon realized our paths had crossed years earlier, back when I had long hair and was living in the yellow house on the other side of town.

She couldn't have known any of this then, at our first date—my history, the origin story of how I arrived in this town via a smaller town, after meeting a couple on the internet who were looking for a live-in housekeeper. I didn't advertise this part on first dates or second dates, just like I wouldn't mention my recent ex-girlfriend.

We went on more dates and texted often, then daily. Being with Lindsay was comfortable—we would talk for hours and listen to records, sharing stories of youthful misadventures and past loves. Lindsay was more cautious than me when it came to making friends and socializing. She liked time alone and had been single—happily so— for several years. After Abbi, I'd jumped right back into dating. The idea of being on my own, uncoupled, was frightening, but I didn't know why, exactly. My body had healed from the treatment, but recovering alone had wounded me, I was fearful of being left again. I needed more care and attention, to feel certain that I was worth staying with.

I told Lindsay about chemo and radiation and the lowest points of recovery. Her eyes welled up as she held my hand. Her compassion was fierce and I could feel it when she held me, when we sat together, bundled up under a blanket, watching the wood stove crackle.

I told her there were two things she needed to know, upfront, if our relationship was going to work long term:

1. I never want kids
2. I am never getting married (again)

I'd had a different view earlier in life, when I married my college girlfriend at age 20—another fact I didn't announce on first dates, because it wasn't relevant. That marriage hadn't lasted; it was doomed to fail, constructed out of a youthful hope, untethered from reality. I was so confident that I missed every warning sign. I did not know myself well enough to be married, and so I promised to never make that mistake again.

Three months in, I was falling in love with Lindsay, even if I wasn't ready to say it out loud. I didn't really mumble, but I was asleep, in the liminal space between conscious and unconscious thought. "I just... love you." There was a kindly emphasis on *love*, like a soothing exhale. I didn't know exactly what had transpired, but when I woke up, she was looking at me, smiling. "I love you too."

She moved in that summer, leaving the small second floor apartment with the tiny kitchen and broken oven. I helped organize and box up her belongings—moving was something she disliked, but I was well practiced and efficient. I labeled boxes: "Kitchen," "Bathroom stuff," "Living room shit." After she'd moved in, she insisted the brown leather couch needed to go. We replaced it with something lighter and more modern. The living room colors too, they could be more welcoming and pleasant. Soon we were planning improvements and making decisions together.

Casual relationships never suited me—Lindsay and I had this in common. There had been flings, but they usually left me wanting. I needed a partnership that was durable. People were starting to use that word when referring to a significant other. My *partner*. I liked how it sounded authoritative, serious like *husband* or *wife*, but non-gendered.

A religious upbringing shaped my early understanding

of how serious relationships were supposed to work. Before cancer, before moving west, I'd left this ideology behind. I wanted a partner and an equal. We would have a shared set of values and goals. I would help them however I could and they would help me too. Lindsay's formative years had also been informed by religion and chaos, in very different ways, but we shared values and goals; we wanted similar things from life and would commit to helping each other. Our relationship, like the paths we had taken to find each other, did not require dogmatic belief. Neither of us had any use for evangelical notions of the ideal relationship—godly, male as the breadwinner and decision maker, children.

The whole persona of godly-male-husband never resonated with me; I could not imagine myself inhabiting the role and the sort of masculinity it demanded. A feeling of difference, of containing another quality, one that was unfamiliar to prototypical men, straight men, had been a part of my life since I was a teenager. I was still that person, still queer, still finding a name for a truth that was interior, newly discovered. Lindsay saw me, as my ex-wife Hillary had, and met my questions—about who I was, what I wanted, how I identified—with kindness. And maybe the whole experience of recovering, from cancer treatment and an abusive relationship, had allowed me to be more aware, more truthful with myself.

My mom claims she knew right away Lindsay was special. My dad once said that she smoothed out my rough edges. I had plenty of unfinished surfaces back then, and still do. The first time I met one of her best friends was at our house, during a party. I was annoyed that she'd brought her toddler. "This is a party, why did she bring her fucking baby?" Lindsay looked right at me: "You are being an asshole. Stop it." I was less measured in those early days, and she was not afraid to check me.

I still spoke to my parents, but not often; our relationship was cordial, if distant. Lindsay gently encouraged me to reach out more often, to call on holidays and birthdays, to send cards with handwritten notes. "Honey... why don't we send your mom a card for Mother's Day?" She was teaching me to be thoughtful and intentional in my relationships, to let go of old grievances.

My skill was solving problems and devising action plans. Early on, Lindsay told me about medical debt that had been following her for many years, now in collections. The overwhelm and shame kept her from dealing with it, so I offered to help. "Here's something to help when you call them back." I gave Lindsay a script I had written, with tips on negotiating down her outstanding debt.

Lindsay did help smooth the edges of a personality that was still a work in progress and her patience was admirable. She helped me become more self-aware, kinder, less judgmental. And I helped her find the confidence she always had, giving her encouragement and gentle nudges when she needed them. The outlines of a life together were beginning to take shape in our 30s. She asked more than once if we could get a dog, but the yard was unfenced, so that needed to happen first, I explained. In truth, I was in no hurry to adopt a pet because the house itself, the constant, ongoing improvement projects, was my pet.

I still thought about flying, though not as much. My time was spent at work and at home—on ladders, in the attic, in the shop—solving problems and improving systems. A new identity was being formed: I was a handyman who happened to also work as a business analyst. I was a homeowner, a problem solver, someone who could deftly manage a project in the physical or digital realm. I was feeling more confident, secure in a career that had momentum, living in a house that was being improved, partnered with someone who loved me.

My work was in the realm of software and I worked on a small team, solving problems, interacting with users and partner organizations. There would be occasional bouts of imposter syndrome, but the work grounded me, I felt useful. I'd found something I was good at and what had been a temp job—something I'd taken to get me by—had turned into a permanent and stable role.

Lindsay's work was in retail, managing people and vendors and schedules for a small grocery store out towards Boston Harbor. She'd been there for nearly a decade and was adored by her customers, but the owners were challenging, the least favorite part of her job. That and the hours, working until 9 pm some nights and the occasional weekend. She wanted to leave and find another job, and I gave her the nudge. She put in her notice at the store and found a part-time gig, working for an online bead retailer, but soon heard about a better paying opportunity working at a trendy salon that offered facials and waxing. I was thrilled to watch as Lindsay made a career change, moving on from a role she'd outgrown, advocating for herself, finding new opportunities.

Maybe I wasn't aware enough to acknowledge it, but I was proud to have come this far, through hard work and plenty of random chance. I had lived through rare cancer and then somehow managed to find a career, and a house, and a loving partner. There was so much to be grateful for but I didn't pause to reflect much back then because pausing was a foreign concept. I needed to keep moving, to do as much as I could *right then*, not later. I'd seen and felt what the end, my end, might be like. After recovering, after leaving Abbi, I dove headlong into change and newness without really considering the significance of my experiences with cancer and how they would continue to change me.

I had so much energy and zeal, determined to create the life that I wanted, that Lindsay wanted. We were figuring out what that was, together. There would be more house projects, maybe a promotion or two, and then in a few years, when things settled down, I would learn to fly. After three years in remission, scans were now once a year. Our trips to Seattle were less frequent and cancer was rarely top of mind, we were past it. I felt incredibly lucky.

It was all going so well and then, a year after she moved in, the runny nose.

Recurrence

The constant drip and endless supply of tissues was the sign, like before. Of course it wasn't allergies. The grasses weren't doing this to me. But maybe I was allergic to *something*. Maybe there was another explanation besides the outcome I'd thought about, often, but tried not to dwell on.

I'd known the likelihood of recurrence was high because I'd read studies on this type of malignancy. But maybe the aggressive treatment put me in a different category. Most of the people diagnosed were older. Many wouldn't have intensive treatment. There was very little data—basically nothing —on what long term looked like for someone diagnosed with sinonasal adenocarcinoma at 30. My cancer friends with more common diseases had a reference point, but I had best guesses.

I went in for scans a month after noticing the runny nose. There was another mass. Dr. Bayles would perform a biopsy to confirm it was cancer, and then remove it surgically. By this time, Dr. Vishnu had already moved on to a clinic in the Midwest, so I met with another oncologist, who explained that I was not a good candidate for chemo or additional radiation.

Based on the outcome from the last round of treatment, there was no reason to believe chemo would be beneficial and the broad spectrum radiation I'd been treated with before was a one-shot sort of thing. I was incredulous. *Really? No treatment options? Nothing?* She suggested I undergo genetic testing, perhaps there were immunotherapy trials that we could explore. No trials or novel therapies existed for my rare cancer.

We drove to Seattle for the outpatient biopsy. Lindsay was in the waiting room and Dr. Bayles found her as I came to in the post-op recovery area. "I wish I had better news for you." Lindsay held back tears as he showed her pictures of the tumor—charred black and tangled purple, embedded in healthy pink and red. Lindsay drove home, my hand on her shoulder. That night before bed, she cried as I held her close. "I don't want you to die. Please don't die."

Recurrence, a concern that had lingered in the background for years, had now become our reality. What would this mean in the long run? Was my life going to be cut short? How could we prevent further spread of this disease if we didn't treat it? I had more questions than my providers had answers and the oncology department at the hospital where I'd started this journey couldn't offer me any solutions. I was determined to do something, to find some sort of treatment.

The surgery was hours behind schedule. Dr. Bayles had another case that pushed mine from morning to late afternoon and I was getting delirious and impatient. Fasting was my least favorite part of this ordeal. The surgery was uneventful—the tumor had been removed with no trouble. Lindsay greeting me as I was wheeled into the hospital room, grinning, eyes wide. "Hi honey! I'm going to have a grilled cheese."

I smiled and laughed but felt guilty—our relationship was still in the early stages and now we were dealing with my cancer. I did not want to be too needy. I'd heard about the Seattle Cancer Care Alliance and I made an appointment with an oncologist there, a specialist in head/neck cancers. Although my case was unusual, Dr. Santana-Davila didn't furrow his brow like Dr. Russell or Dr. Bayles. He seemed confident that a newer, more precise form of radiation could give me the best chance at success: Proton therapy. This form of radiation was delivered with greater precision, which in turn meant milder side effects, and hopefully, a curative outcome.

After the surgery, we had a follow up with Dr. Bayles. I explained that I was looking into proton treatment. He scoffed.

"If you have an expensive radiation machine and a whole center built around it, the doctors are going to find ways to make sure it gets used."

I was surprised at his opinion and his openness in sharing it, normally our appointments were genial but brief, and he never had much to say. But I was completely undeterred. The new oncologist was more specialized and they had recommended a course of action—something was going to be done, which was better than doing nothing.

I was going to have proton radiation treatment and blast the remaining cancer cells to oblivion in a more targeted way than before. And then maybe, finally, we could be done with this cancer business. Diagnosis then aggressive and broad treatment, followed by recurrence with targeted treatment. My doctors were confident—and so was I—this was the best pathway to a cure.

More treatment meant more time in Seattle. Lindsay mentioned the possibility of time off for my treatment to her new boss and then, suddenly, performance-related concerns surfaced. Lindsay was fired weeks before I was set to begin another round of treatment. She was devastated. I held her as she cried—none of this was fair. How could her boss be so cold? I remembered the shock of being let go from the internet company.

"It's going to be okay sweetie, also—fuck her—you deserve better."

I would be going through cancer treatment again, three years after my experience with chemo and radiation, when I'd suffered profoundly. I had been alone then, which compounded the pain. But Lindsay was here now, and wanted to be with me. She cried for the job loss and cried for the cancer. I tried to encourage her.

"It's going to be better this time—I know it."

I didn't know what treatment would be like, not exactly, but I did have a reference point for pain—the unrelenting kind that hollows you out, body and self. I would not want to repeat that experience, nor would I wish it on anyone, but I had lived through it. I'd recovered. And this new protocol —just radiation, no chemotherapy—was going to be easier.

Even though I had cancer again, I wasn't going to be alone. Lindsay's presence was reassuring—she wanted to be with me during cancer treatment—and I felt safe knowing that whatever the outcome, we would have each other. None of this was ideal, but we would get through it.

A sister of a friend let us stay in their mother-in-law suite, a little apartment above their garage, which was near the treatment center. I wouldn't need to take long bus rides —I could walk or bike. I decided that I would continue to work full time.

Treatments were twice a day during the week, morning and afternoon. The waiting area was big and bright, with the names of donors on gold-plated placards. Many of the patients were kids, some toddlers, with shaved heads. Proton therapy was useful for treating brain tumors it seemed.

As before, I had a custom headpiece made, in light green plastic mesh. The molded headgear snapped onto the table, ensuring perfect alignment every time I would lie on the table and receive my dose of protons.

I started working remotely for the first time. The owners of the mother-in-law, set back from their new and modern house, were a nurse and architect. The space was full of building designs, blueprints, and framed art. I set up my workstation on an old drafting table and imagined I was creating something as useful as a building, sketching ideas and process flows on sheets of graph paper.

We slept on an air mattress and the kitchen was down-stairs, next to the garage. A fabric curtain hid the toilet and shower. My days began earlier than before. I made coffee and then started in on work. Treatments were usually done by 5 pm and then we'd go explore the neighborhood.

We walked to pubs and restaurants, sampled local brew-eries, holding hands as we navigated broken sidewalks. I only had to do this for eight weeks and that was it. There were virtually no side effects, until we were a month in. A familiar sensitivity in my mouth and throat had returned, but it was manageable, not catastrophic like before. I could still eat, I wasn't in pain, I just needed to get creative with food, so I wouldn't lose too much weight.

Broth, beer, and protein packed smoothies were the main food groups—ramen too, which was my usual lunch and dinner when I was eating alone. We went to the Asian supermarket and found all manner of noodles, adding new salty flavors to my spartan radiation diet.

On days when I walked from the treatment center back to the mother-in-law, I'd sometimes take a detour through the nearby cemetery. I wasn't thinking about death, or flying, but I was missing our home in Olympia and the familiar, everyday things. I thought about the first time, how I'd stayed in a rented room not too far from here. Abbi never stayed with me. We didn't go on walks. She didn't have the ability to support me and I managed, for a while. *I am doing this all over again, but I am not alone.*

I was given a medallion and a certificate when treatment ended, like I'd won some sort of prize. We packed up the mother-in-law and headed home.

Boulder

In the space of a month or two, I was fully recovered, with a mouth restored to normal function. My attention returned to house projects. I was in remission, having treated the cancer in my face with targeted, strategic protons. Life was back to normal. We booked a trip to Colorado to visit my brother and some of Lindsay's friends.

My younger brother Tim knew about my flying dreams. He was deep into his medical residency in Denver, but still took the time to find an instructor nearby who'd give us a half day of training—with the chance to fly solo. From an early age, Tim was an adventurer, fearless in his desire to explore; once, barely four years old, he managed to open the garage door to our house in the suburbs and went on a self-guided trek on a nearby trail, red wagon in tow. Tim still navigated trails, on his mountain bike, when he wasn't caring for patients, working the unforgiving hours demanded of residents.

We meet the instructor, Misha, just before sunrise. We were going to fly if the conditions were right. He hands us bulky rucksacks with shoulder straps and the hike up begins. My brother proceeded with little effort as I lagged behind a bit, knees aching. I was not in top hiking shape anymore. Treatment had been easier the second time around but I'd been losing the wellspring of energy I'd had as a younger person. My pace was slowing.

The trail was all red, dry dirt, with switchbacks and prickly plants. To the west was a ridge—beneath it, east, an open field with a green park. The plan was to hike part of the way up. We hiked for nearly an hour and then finally set our gear on the ground. We were prepared to learn the basics of paragliding, just enough so we could safely launch and land in the park below.

We watched as Misha unfolded one of the wings, explaining the anatomy of the glider—the cells of the canopy that would fill with air, the front leading edge where the air would enter, the lines and risers that connected the wing to the harness. I was baffled at how many thin bits of material there were. How would you keep track of everything? How did one prevent them from getting all tangled, like loose cords in a backpack?

Misha donned a harness and illustrated how the leg and chest straps would connect and then helped us repeat the process, snapping buckles, checking them, attaching the risers from the wing to carabiners on the harness. The flight plan was simple—run forward to inflate the glider, keep running until airborne, and then follow our instructor's commands on the radio. We took turns practicing the launch technique, lines and controls draped over our forearms, arms extended with elbows slightly bent, almost at a right angle but not quite.

The hill was an advantage. With the glider laid out

above, uphill, the force needed to pull forward and inflate the wing was manageable. I was surprised by how heavy it felt—more like pulling a wheelbarrow than throwing a sheet over a bed. In skydiving, the force of falling at over 100 mph causes your parachute to inflate in mere seconds; I'd never considered what it would feel like to catch the air, moving on the ground, with a bundle of fabric. The air had weight and mass because it was made of particles, gases and the like, but this was always theoretical, never experiential. I felt the actual substance of the air that day, as I pulled the glider overhead and moved my body in concert with it.

I agree to launch first, because Tim insists. "Come on bro, you go." Tim knew I'd been thinking, dreaming—at times mildly obsessing—about paragliding ever since I discovered it. I stand with the lines across my arms, controls in hand, nervous but nothing like the skydives. The stakes felt lower. We were on a modest hill, not in an airplane at 12,000 feet. The morning was quiet and calm and there was no rush—I could launch at my own pace, when I was ready.

Tim is standing behind me. My shoulders are forward as I run, just like we'd practiced, and I feel the weight of the wing pull against me. I lean further forward, into the harness, tucking my chin slightly. I'm running with a tether and a weight behind, steadily moving forward, not sprinting but almost jogging. The wing is overhead and the center of gravity has shifted. I'm not pulling anymore. I'm running beneath the wing and it's moving with me. Only a few steps more and I am no longer touching the ground. I've left.

I was surprised at how simple this sort of flying is. The hike had been more of a challenge than launching, and flying—actually controlling this aircraft made of fabric—was easy. I realize my flight is going to be short, but right now time is elongated because all of this is new, like when I first learned to ride a bike. I know that I am going to want more.

I am flying. This is exactly like flying the parachute, but slower and more deliberate. The air is moving around my face and into this wing and we are moving together. I am being carried, held by the air. I make the turn right when I'm told. The park is close and I'm not very high. I can see people hiking up the trail and a bunch of folks with gliders in the park, they seem to be practicing. I am above the grassy area, closer to the ground now. I pull the controls in a firm, fluid motion, down past my hips. I'm in a seated position and then I'm sliding onto the soft grass. The wing deflates into a crumpled tangle of fabric and cords.

Tim is about to launch because I can hear the radio check. I'm standing in the park, looking up, trying to take a zoomed-in video. There was some wind, but not much. The wing is overhead and he's being told to run, and then "hands up, hands up." He's left the ground and is turning as the glider pitches like a top. He's tracking to the right, towards the trail we'd hiked, away from the park. The instructor directs him to adjust course. My brother waits and then finally changes direction after the command is repeated. Tim is more accustomed to giving instructions. He is back on the correct heading, approaching the grassy field at the edge of the park. He flies near where I am standing. "Okay, ready... " He lands safely, sliding then standing.

After years of waiting, cancer and treatment, recurrence and treatment again, I have finally flown a paraglider. The instructor packs up the gliders and gear, and I ask about learning to fly. He mentions connections to a school in Santa Barbara but is not aware of instructors closer to me, in Washington. The dream was more tangible now—I had flow an actual paraglider, from a hill down into a park. The universe of the sport was still completely foreign to me but I was sold, more than after the skydives, when my only reference was watching other people fly on YouTube. Now it was a thing I had actually done. I would be more steadfast. I would learn how to fly and I would do it as soon as possible. There was momentum now and the dream was finally coming into view.

ORN

We returned from the mini-vacation in Colorado and settled back into the routines of the week—house projects and all the rest. I told everyone at work about my introductory flight, how I'd finally tried paragliding after years of dreaming about it. My office was about a mile from the house, and most days I'd walk or ride my bike. After work, I'd come home and spend another three to four hours on house projects. My energy level could sustain this sort of pace. I was always moving, doing something with my hands, when I wasn't enmeshed in the technical details of my day job.

I started taking naps every so often; I was working constantly, and maybe I was getting burned out. Some days I would come home at lunchtime and rest for ten minutes, lying down in bed, but just briefly. I'd wake up feeling more energized, ready to continue on with the day. Over the next several months, the naps stopped working. I was still tired, more tired than I expected to be at 4 pm, when I would usually walk home from work. Something was off.

What felt like occasional fatigue was turning into a different sort of problem. Maintaining focus was becoming a challenge. Speech, at times, was difficult to decipher, as if the person in front of me—usually my coworker, sometimes Lindsay—was speaking in a foreign language and I'd lost the ability to translate their words. This might only last for mere moments, and then the light would flicker back on and I could understand again. I'd never had problems with my vision, but when this would happen, my sensory grid would go offline for a few seconds, and everything was blurry. I'd close my eyes tightly and then blink them open, bringing everything back into focus.

I started getting headaches, which was unusual. I'd never had migraines, or chronic pain beyond knees that would ache now and again. The decline was slow, almost imperceptible. I started taking naps after work, in addition to rests at lunch. The ache in my head started to become more severe. Waves of pain would start in my head and then saturate my body, bathing me in awful static. There was no way I could be a productive person if this continued.

In the spring, we were back in Seattle for more scans. I didn't have cancer again, which was a relief, but this new problem was more disruptive than malignant tumors. I couldn't function normally. I couldn't do my job well and I had no energy to fix the house. I was feeling something like depression, mixed with anger and guilt. I needed to be able to work, in part because I loved working, being productive, doing and making and designing. If I couldn't put my energy into something I loved, then what would become of my life?

I was mad at my body and upset that I couldn't work at 100%. I had no idea what chronic pain was like. Chemo and radiation, that first time around, were debilitating for a while, but then I recovered. The impact was acute, but temporary. This pain would not go away. I was losing my focus, my hobbies, the energy to be the person I was familiar with. Whatever this condition, it was changing me, stripping away my identity.

Dr. Kirtland was a specialist in treating pain, with decades of experience; he was genial and spoke softly, looking at me directly, hands clasped. We talked about the nature of my pain, my history of cancer and treatments. Opioids were an option, one that could bring me relief, but he was clear—once that door was opened, it was difficult to close. I remembered the high-powered pain meds after chemo and decided to confront the pain rather than living in that sort of fog again. He recommended nerve pain medication, giving that a try first, and increasing the dose over time. Drugs in this category, anticonvulsants, work by targeting a different set of receptors than opioids, ones that are not connected to the feelings of euphoria. This sounded more reasonable—there was less risk of long-term dependency. Dr. Kirtland also referred me to another pain specialist who led something like a group therapy session for people with chronic pain. I was ready to try anything, except opioids.

The nerve pain drug helped for a while. I was supplementing it with ibuprofen—800 mg a day at first, then 1200, 1600, then even more, approaching double the recommended dose. My nose would bleed randomly because I was basically taking a massive amount of blood thinners. Still working full time, I was convinced whatever this problem was, it was temporary. I was so lucky to have my job, to have finally found a career. The timing had been improbable; my cancer diagnosis came five months after starting. I felt a debt of gratitude towards this company, and the people in it, who kept me on despite all of the unknowns. I was not accustomed to being valued in this way. And so I'd decided I would prove myself, by working as hard as I could.

I simply needed to find the right meds at the proper dose to control the pain, probably from nerve damage caused by cancer treatment. That was the likely explanation —and meds would eventually ease the radiation-induced nerve pain.

My sense of smell had been gone for five years, but the loss early on had been gradual. I was accustomed to explaining this fact, whenever someone would look at me and ask "Hey, did you smell that?", or make a comment on whatever delicious food I was eating.

"No, I don't have a sense of smell. Because of cancer."

Often, this was met with an apology.

"Oh... I didn't know, I'm sorry", someone might say, as if I had some sort of debilitating disease.

I didn't mind living without smells—it was a superpower sometimes. I could be around the most putrid scents, completely unfazed, smells that would make most people wretch and gag. Fart smells didn't even register, which was very funny at home. I'd laugh and laugh as Lindsay pinched her nose.

I worked in the office most days, back when attire was less casual—button ups, slacks, the occasional jacket for high-profile meetings. I met with my boss on a weekly basis. She was an achiever, a climber, someone who prioritized her career growth above other matters. My work, my team's work, was usually an afterthought. But I was glad to be there, content in my role, and generally tried to steer clear of politics and management.

It was early in the work day, mid-morning, and I was tired but not in the fog of exhaustion; the new meds were helping. I was sitting at my desk, headphones on, listening to music as I worked. She called me into her office. I was confused because this wasn't our normal check-in day. Something was amiss. Sitting down, she explained there had been a complaint. About me. *Oh really? This is going to be interesting.* I had been watching my mouth ever since dropping an f-bomb in a meeting, but that was years ago, well before she was my boss. So what the fuck could this *complaint* be?

"We've received reports about a smell, your smell. Are your clothes getting washed?" she asked, looking past me.

My face was probably turning red at this point, from anger and embarrassment mixed with a load of confusion. I didn't know how to respond but I knew I wanted this conversation to end, right now. I wanted to run out of her office and go home and be done for the day. I could barely remember what a bad smell was because I lacked the ability to perceive them, like a high pitched tone outside the range of human hearing. Despite the deficit, I still wore deodorant, I knew that smells were real to most people. I clenched my teeth, nodded, trying not to speak.

"Mmhmm. Okay, I get it."

She thanked me and I walked out of the office, humiliated.

My clothes were not dirty. I relayed the incident to Lindsay at home later that day and she was incensed.

"I wash your clothes, so they aren't *dirty*."

She took great pride in the laundry, her favorite chore. I

asked if she had any idea why someone would complain about me smelling bad.

"Well... sometimes there is a smell. Not always though."

She knew, but hadn't said anything too direct about it. Lindsay was afraid I'd be upset, offended by something I was incapable of experiencing. She explained it wasn't a constant problem—some days there was a smell and other days there wasn't. And she couldn't tell where it was coming from, maybe my mouth—bad breath perhaps? Gingivitis? She'd kept quiet about it until now, as I'm indignantly recalling the conversation where my boss had the nerve to suggest that I wore stinky clothes to work. We would need to figure this out. I was in constant pain and now there was a foul smell emanating from my face.

I figured the pain in my head and sometimes my mouth was a dental issue. I saw my dentist and explained the mouth pain. He examined my teeth and noticed a molar that was in rough shape—it would need to come out. I'd had a molar or two extracted before, so I was not alarmed. As long as my front teeth and my smile were in good shape, I didn't care. My dentist extracted the tooth, and felt the sound of bone breaking apart like the crushing of a soda can. Maybe this was the problem all along, a stupid tooth.

But the pain continued and I then started waking up at night, unable to sleep with daggers in the back of my head. I made an appointment with Dr. Bayles. He'd been involved in my care since the beginning and might be able to offer some guidance on the pain and the smell. The last time I'd seen him—the runny nose, the recurrence—he'd removed the tumor, but had nothing to offer me in terms of treatment, no plan to prevent the cancer's return. I wanted a clear answer, an option, but back then his input hadn't been very helpful. Now I had a new problem and wanted a curative solution. I hadn't yet realized just how nebulous and complicated this whole thing was going to be

Dr. Bayles look over my most recent scans and then scoped me. He explained that I had developed an infection, along with a fistula—an opening between my mouth and sinuses that wasn't supposed to be there—likely caused by the pulled tooth. We had created a new problem trying to solve another.

Dr. Bayles explained that repairing the fistula surgically was possible, but too risky, given the amount of radiation I'd been exposed to. There was a significant chance the surgery would fail and cause further problems. But, there was a treatment option that could help with the pain and potentially close the fistula. Dr. Bayles mentioned something called hyperbaric oxygen, a specialized treatment used for chronic wounds that won't heal and other conditions like the bends, which divers can get when surfacing too quickly. I was ready to try anything.

Dr. Bayles prescribed liquid antibiotics for the infection, which I would add to my saline rinses, in an effort to address the smell. We visited the hyperbaric clinic, which was underwater themed. In the waiting room was a large tank with exotic fish. I appreciated the bright colors set against blue hues; the clinic felt more like a park than a treatment center. The chamber where we would do our 'dives' looked like a half-finished submarine. The treatments would last about 90 minutes, the technician explained. I would be in the tubular chamber with other patients as the pressure was gradually increased, until we were at 2.4 atmospheres, the equivalent of being about fifty feet underwater. Then, we'd don clear plastic full-head helmets, which would deliver pure oxygen. The general idea was that the combination of pressure and oxygen kickstarted healing processes, hopefully helping to regrow vessels in tissues damaged by radiation.

It was springtime in 2020, I'd just turned 36, and everyone I knew was uncertain about this virus we were hearing about on the news. I would begin treatments in May —forty dives in all. There was no traffic on I-5 early on. Every Monday, Wednesday, and Friday, we would leave around 5:30 am. I drove northbound because Lindsay was not, and is not, a morning person. The clinic staff wore masks and we did too. The routine became a ritual and a time trial. *Arrive, locker room, medium scrubs, book in hand, wait until called.* As the chamber pressurized, the air would heat up; we were beginning our descent in this big metal pipe of a ship. Everyone had recliners, and the technicians would watch us as we dove further down. Mouths opened and ears popped, some people chewed gum to help equalize the pressure. The chamber creaked and clanked as air moved against metal like a high-tech steam engine. Once the headgear was on, no one could hear each other, so a solitary activity was ideal. Lindsay sat in the waiting room reading her own book and I was in the chamber reading mine.

Depressurizing, the opposite of diving would happen, and slowly. If it didn't, if you came up too quickly, you'd get the bends, like a deep sea diver. The air was cold for a few moments as the depth gauge moved like the second hand on a clock; we were approaching sea level again. The technician would get up and the metal slab door creaked open. Lindsay would drive home, southbound. Our summer was spent this way—driving and diving, reading books and waiting, hoping I was healing, with no way of seeing progress.

After finishing forty dives, the pandemic was wide-spread and I was still in pain. The hyperbaric treatments had not solved the problem, the pain or the fistula. The medicated saline rinses had fixed the smell, which mattered less because I was working at home. Dr. Bayles had recommended that I do more frequent debridements, so I made an appointment with a local ENT, Dr. Jung. We were sick of driving to Seattle, even with nil traffic. I wondered if this was the solution, more frequent nasal deep cleanings.

Dr. Jung worked in the same office as the recently retired Dr. Russell. *Good for him*, I thought. Jung sprayed the nasty lidocaine before scoping and scraping. He was young, but measured, and maybe he thought he was out of his depth after reading my chart. He said I should see a colleague of his, someone he trusted and respected. They could probably offer me better advice about what was happening and what options I might have. I did not have a plan or any clue about what would follow, but I knew that I could not live a normal life in this state.

The first year of the pandemic was coming to an end and we were back in Seattle. The traffic was worse, the pain too, despite the dives and new meds, cleanings and rinses. I stopped seeing the pain clinic provider but enrolled in a research study she'd recommended: chronic pain management using guided meditation. Every day, sometimes twice, I would lie on the bed and listen to a woman's voice. I focused my attention on my toes, my knees, hips, and chest. I took deep breaths and relaxed until my body was warm putty. This actually helped. I would get up and return to whatever I was doing with more energy. The pain was not out in front anymore, it was somewhere else. I didn't need to give it so much room. If I couldn't make it go away completely, maybe I could change the way I thought about it.

Meditation was helpful but it wasn't a long-term solution. We met Dr. Abuzeid and I began to tell him my cancer story from the start: the diagnosis, surgery, chemo and radiation, recurrence a few years later followed by my surgery and radiation. And then we talked about the reason I was there in Seattle—unrelenting pain. I was blanketed in it and had trouble recalling when it started because I had adjusted, so I could work.

But that was all I could do—work—because there was no energy left for anything else. I could smile and maintain the composure I needed to get through the day and then I would collapse. Every day I would focus, summoning all of the energy I could find and point it at work. There would be no chance of flying unless we fixed whatever was causing this. Dr. Abuzeid wanted to confer with a team of his colleagues about my case. I would need to come back for more imaging and then we could discuss next steps.

The scan confirmed his suspicion—significant parts of my upper jaw and skull had deteriorated from radiation damage. I'd developed a condition called osteoradionecrosis, essentially bone death from radiation exposure. This was a risk you'd hear about before starting treatment, one that doesn't really register because the singular focus is dealing with the cancer. I was not worried about what might happen later, because there might not be a later if we didn't deal with the cancer now.

We had been trying everything and nothing was working because the damage had accumulated over time, radiation quietly destroying pieces that held my face together. There was no reversing this process once it started, it was permanent, not like a wound or a broken bone. Saving the damaged areas of my skull would be impossible. I wasn't shocked, not exactly; I felt a sense of relief, finally having a name for what was happening to me. I'd been reliving a version of my experience with the runny nose prior to diagnosis, the discomfort and not-knowing, just orders of magnitude worse.

My relationship with surgery was about to change. I was no stranger to scans, scopes, biopsies, and surgical excisions. I'd had tumors removed twice and I tolerated anesthesia well. In fact, I enjoyed being put under—it was a little break from consciousness that reminded me how amazing life was when I became a person again. The surgeries were all about taking out the cancer, cutting just enough around the tumor, taking some good tissue too, lowering the odds that it would regrow. Each time I recovered—which never took very long and I would return to my life, body basically the same as before.

It was a dark and rainy morning when we drove back to Seattle in early 2021 for a follow-up appointment. The scans had provided direct proof of what Dr. Abuzeid had suspected and now it was time to talk options. We didn't meet with Dr. Abuzeid though, the leading role for my care had been handed to Dr. Barber, her expertise more closely aligned with my case. No one was shaking hands then so we greeted each other with outstretched palms and a gentle half wave. "I am so sorry this is happening to you," she said, looking at me and then at Lindsay. My medical chart was up on a screen, but she was looking at us directly.

We only saw her eyes, seemingly forlorn, disappointed

that someone so young—her age—was dealing with the aftermath of cancer and cancer treatment. And now there were second-order effects. We were trying to fix damage caused by the treatment, which had created a new and more challenging problem, instead of curing the disease. We were in the territory of bad outcomes, and dealing with them would require drastic measures.

Dr. Barber explained that the area of my skull base, which was now exposed, was close to an important artery, the internal carotid. Keeping this fragile vessel safe was extremely important—damage from infection or a tumor could mean a swift end. I would likely bleed out in minutes, before an ambulance or hospital could help. Of course this was speculative, but the risk was real, and while the antibiotics had helped with the bad smell it was still there, lingering, likely the result of all the decay.

Lindsay and I listened as she described the surgery to address the rot and the pain. Dr. Barber, along with a team of surgeons, would take a piece of my left arm—vessels and flesh I would donate to myself—and use it to cover the area of concern, performing what is known as a free flap reconstruction. They would sow and attach part of my own body into a place it didn't really belong to prevent damage to the more vulnerable interior. My neck would need to be opened too, because this donated tissue would require a blood supply, which would come from larger veins and arteries. Before this transplantation would happen, they would remove all of the damaged bone, a segment of my skull about the size of an orange slice, and with it, the lingering radiation.

This was more complex than I expected and I struggled to visualize it. What would my arm be like afterwards?

Would it work the same? I wanted to see the steps that were needed to do something like this. I was surprised it was even possible. And what about recovery? My only reference was a nasty bout of chemo and relatively simple tumor excisions. A multi-stage head/neck reconstruction was not comparable and I needed to sit and think before deciding.

Lindsay and I talked about the prospect of major surgery that would require hospitalization and extended recovery. I'd never spent more than a night in the hospital before— most of my surgeries had involved just a few hours in the OR—and now we were looking at eight, ten, maybe more, given the complexity of reconstruction. I worried about extended recovery, not knowing what that meant in the context of surgery. I thought about what this would mean for work, for Lindsay; she was adamant I *would* take ample time off and she assured me she'd be there to help. She also knew that I would have difficulty lying around, that I would want to be up and moving—doing something, anything—as soon as I could.

Dr. Barber called a few days later. There weren't any questions left to answer, just a decision to make. We were going to take action; I was going to proceed with the flap surgery. A cascade of planning followed. I would need to be hospitalized for at least a week, which meant leave from work and a full pause on everything else. Lindsay and I conferred about how friends and family would be informed of my status during and after surgery. My coworkers sent well wishes and notes, along with gift cards for take-out and home improvement supplies, something for me to look forward to once recovered. The flurry of concern and curiosity was encouraging and it fueled my interest in learning all I could about this procedure. I read everything I

could find—surgical planning guidelines, animated train-
ings, a video of an actual flap harvest. Knowing and seeing
the reality of this surgery was reassuring.

What was about to happen was highly specialized and
multidisciplinary, but it wasn't experimental. Flap proce-
dures, and the radial forearm in particular, were broadly
used in the field of reconstructive surgery. I liked having
these facts and holding them tight. What was less common,
was using a forearm flap to do a reconstruction on the upper
part of my jaw the radiation had destroyed. I learned there
were unique risks and considerations, things that made this
rebuild precarious. The flap or structures surrounding it
could fail, necessitating more surgery. I could develop a
cerebrospinal fluid leak, which could prevent the flap from
covering the vital internal carotid artery. And every risk was
compounded by the nature of facial anatomy, the tight
spaces Dr. Barber and her team would be working in, and
the increased risk of infection from radiation-damaged
tissue and bone.

Dr. Barber was taking the lead because she had the skills
and experience to orchestrate the entire effort. There were
other surgeons involved in an undertaking of this magnitude and everyone needed to work in careful coordination,
making decisions along the way that would impact the
outcome, my life. Some part of the work, in reconstructive
surgery, is by necessity exploratory. There was an element of
the unknown that would require decisions and adjustments
to the plan, which are hidden from view, obscured by layers
of skin and fascia and bone. I was going to entrust Dr.
Barber and her team with my face. I had never seen hers,
except in a headshot on the University's website, but her
eyes told the story of who she was. This woman would take

care of my face and help repair the damage. There was no way to prepare beyond learning and trusting, just like the first skydive and the flight to the park.

We arrived at the hospital well before sunrise. A new COVID outbreak meant that less critical surgeries were being delayed. I was going to stay in the hospital for a while, because this was more than a simple tumor excision; I was about to undergo a complicated and risky reconstructive surgery, and because of the pandemic, I'd be in the hospital alone.

Reconstruction

Flap 1

I am waiting in pre-op alone, texting Lindsay and my brother Tim. There's a little current of excitement from all of the anticipation. *I don't actually mind having surgery, and isn't it lovely to be around all of these people?* I greet the nurses and residents and anesthesia folks with enthusiasm. They smile, moving energetically; I imagine their shifts have just started. I am positive and upbeat. I have committed to doing this and I am ready, as prepared as anyone can be to have part of their face rebuilt with a chunk of their arm. The bed in pre-op has a space-age warming blanket with a warm air machine attached. I am so very cozy and relaxed. My breathing is measured and I'm paying attention to it. There are so many residents. My brother would have interesting things to say if he was here, now that he's been practicing medicine for a while.

I sign the informed consent. Dr. Barber is here and we're almost ready. She's in scrubs, wearing one of those surgeon's hats that looks like a shorter version of a chef's hat. Everyone leaves and then the anesthesiologist shows up. I tell him I'm an easy patient—because I am—where sedation is concerned. He's wheeling me down corridors, around turn corners, past other patients in beds, waiting in hallways. We stop outside the OR, the one Dr. Barber will command. The bed is wheeled in, next to a table, and a couple of people lift the sheets under me, hoisting me off the bed and onto the table. I am cold for a moment as the space-age warm air machine is briefly turned off and on again, and now I'm being fitted with leg-squeezing wraps, secured with velcro. There is an imposing circular light above me and a dozen people all moving around in preparation for the main event. I want to thank everyone but now I have an oxygen mask instead of a fabric one. Dr. Barber is at my side. She holds my hand for a moment. "We are going to take good care of you" are the words I remember. My arm is tingling as the first sedative flows through the IV in my hand. I'm counting down. *Ten... nine...*

I'm awake and alive and no time has passed at all, even though people are texting me and saying it's the next day. *WRONG!* I am in such a good mood. This surgery was a breeze, I knew it would be. I bet Lindsay would love a selfie of me right now. Perfect, I'll take a few then. We're in... a recovery room? Everyone is talking but not really making a lot of sense unless they speak slowly while looking right at me. The physical therapist is here for some reason. Oh, they want to make sure I can still walk. Ha! Of course I can walk. Walking is as easy as it's ever been, I'm a little wobbly, but the only reason is all these drugs they have me on. I'm back in my bed and it's cozy and I have a button I can press if I feel pain. I feel something but I can't make out the substance of it—a tightness, an ache maybe; it's far away and I'd like to keep it like that. Click. *Mmmm, Dilaudid.* My blood feels so warm and I love to smile. I'm going to text my family and say something funny. I tell them I've left the hospital on a Segway, heading towards downtown Seattle. Saying this isn't crazy, it's funny as hell. There's no need for me to stay in the hospital for very long, I'm feeling just fine. I should make sure Dr. Barber knows so she can discharge me early.

By the time I'm out of recovery and in my hospital room, where I'll stay for a week, this is no longer fun. My nose has a tube in it, which is uncomfortable, and there's a bit of plastic that's sutured in place, which seems unnecessary and cruel. There's no way for me to sleep with nurses bugging me every few hours. But I'm resolved to have a positive attitude and be a good patient. I am so dreadfully tired and my face is sore. My arm is bandaged up with a drain in it, collecting blood in a little soft plastic pouch. The residents come around every so often to mess with a sensor embedded in my neck that is monitoring blood flow to my new flap. The nurses empty the drain in my arm and another one in my neck.

My face is swollen and I look like shit. I look ugly—no more selfies. I hope they can take out this stupid nose tube and let me eat some real food. The residents tell me we need to wait because we don't want to disrupt the flap so early in this stage of healing. *Okay, that makes sense.* Taking a shit here is awful because I'm on a liquid diet and there is no bidet, like at home. I can't wait to be in my bed and get some decent sleep.

The residents are back and they tell me the neck sensor can come out—progress! I can feel the wires buried in my neck being pulled out in one swift motion. There's no pain, just a strange and brief feeling of revulsion, as this mechanical device emerges from a hole in my skin, my body's way of saying *thank you, this does not belong here.* I see my arm, my forever modified left arm. The incision runs all the way up to my elbow and there's a skin graft over the site of the harvested flap. The grafted skin, from my left thigh, is translucent and perforated, surrounded by sutures.

Five days have gone by, six if you include the time I spent in the OR, and I'm finally changing out of this ill-fitting hospital gown and into my own clothes. I've been cleared to leave. My voice is different, too nasal, weirdly pitched, and my arm feels taut like a snare drum. I try to reassure myself that this is only temporary, that I will sound familiar again, more like the self I know. I need some real sleep, but I don't want rest for more than a day or two because I'm eager to do something, anything, after spending days and days lying in a hospital bed with crummy pillows. I couldn't read because of the brain fog and talking on the phone was too much of a challenge with the feeding tube.

I decide that recovery means building something made from wood, something durable and useful. I rested at home for two days—Lindsay insisted—but there is no reason to rest more. Ready to be active and creative, I decide I will design and build a desk. Sketching and measuring, cutting and sanding, I am in the familiar space of my shop, unconcerned about how I look now, the puffy cheeks and jaw, the gash in my neck. I am relieved that my arm works just fine. The skin will feel strange for a while, but I haven't lost anything. This surgery merely rearranged some parts, with no discernible impact on function. Dr. Barber told me things might change, but they haven't, not really—I am so relieved. I'm not sure I could handle an outcome that was more drastic, a disability, a permanent loss. The dull haze of the pain meds is gone and my mind and body are working. I am comfortable, I like who I am.

My arm was healing and the incision in my neck was reforming into a scar, but my voice was still off. Dr. Barber said it might take a few weeks, after the swelling had subsided, for it to sound more normal. Two weeks passed and I used a get-well gift card to buy new clamps for my shop. I could eat some solid foods now but liquids were starting to exit my nose. The section of my palate that had been opened for the surgery and sown back together was starting to separate, splitting like a snake's tongue. Talking was increasingly difficult, alienating; the sounds coming from my own mouth were unrecognizable. I could not summon enough breath to form whole words, air escaping through a widening hole, sounds muffled and distorted. We saw Dr. Barber again. The flap had been a success, it was healthy still, but my palate was rapidly deteriorating.

The surgery had caused a cascade, accelerating a failure that was already underway, and now my palate was in full collapse. The only solution: another, more extensive flap surgery, using muscle from my left thigh. There was more damage and rot to remove and now my smile was at risk. I would probably loose a tooth or two. We had discussed this possibility and I was more alarmed at the idea of sacrificing my teeth than donating my leg muscle. How could I live a normal life with a failing voice *and* a fractured smile? How would I work? Dr. Barber said the surgery scheduler would call us soon, which usually meant a few days. My phone rang as we rolled out of the subterranean parking lot. The surgery would be in three days, less than a month after the first flap reconstruction.

I wasn't excited anymore, I wasn't hopeful. I was defeated. I didn't sign up for multiple rounds. My big, complicated surgery was supposed to be a one-time thing, and then, after a longer than usual recovery, we'd move on; the pain would be resolved and I'd have some crazy scars and that would be it. But nothing is ever that simple. This is the lesson I couldn't seem to learn.

Flap 2

I was drained, emotionally, from trying to speak and being upset at the sound I heard. *That is not me.* I started to wonder who I was, exactly, if my voice was never the same again. My body had not changed like this before. Sure, my nasal passageways were cavernous, but that was hidden from view, something only ENTs and radiologists would notice. My voice was my self. This was the person I'd been living as for thirty-six years and now that was all going to be upended. I would need to learn who I was, again, but I barely had time to think before I was in pre-op, waiting, alone.

Dr. Barber said my left leg would work a little different after this flap surgery. It might be weaker and some of my activities would need to change as I recovered. Unlike the first surgery, this one was a multi-step process that would require another surgery six-to-eight months later. The leg muscle would be harvested, more of the damaged jaw bone and palate removed, and then the flap would be used to create a new palate. As before, my neck would be opened up so this second flap could be vascularized, given blood flow from nearby vessels. And once this stage of the process was done, once I'd fully healed and the flap was secure, I'd come back for another surgery to trim it back, cutting the thick muscle down to a more manageable size. This whole ordeal was complicated and risky when we were talking about one flap surgery. Now we would compound the risk with another, less than a month after the first.

I was less effervescent but still polite with the nurses and residents as I waited in pre-op. My forearm no longer needed bandages but the scars were fresh and bright. The nurse asked so I explained I'd had flap surgery recently but needed another. I felt defeated, resigned to an outcome I didn't want for a problem I didn't cause.

I was ready for another surgery but not happy about it. I didn't want this, to be here, in a hospital again. My face still looks uneven and I just want my voice to be fixed—why is that so goddamn difficult? I'm disappointed and a little angry that I let myself believe, again, that I'd found a simple solution, a cure, to my problem. That first surgery was supposed to be it—I was supposed to get the fistula and the smell resolved in one go, but here we are again, more damage and more repairs.

Dr. Barber is here as the anesthesia guy prepares to suspend my consciousness. She holds my hand. I see her eyes and know she does not want this either.

My eyes are open and I cannot breathe. I am gasping, dying probably. Someone get this thing out of my throat and now. I can't move and the room is a blur. *Why am I in this place?* It looks like a sci-fi movie, blue light and endless rows of people in beds, but no one is awake except me. I've woken from the anesthesia, something like thirty hours later, and

I'm still intubated. My eyes are panicked, trying to find someone to help me. I'm moving around, trying to say something while also choking. After more time than I wish to remember, two people are standing over me and the choking hazard is pulled out of my throat. That didn't feel good but at least I can breathe again. They give me drugs and I'm calmer.

I don't want to move because everything is pain. The nurses are wheeling me somewhere and now there's a clear, thin tube. Oh no, not this. Please. The nasogastric tube is how I'll be receiving nutrition; I would rather have another hole in my stomach. The nurse is trying to slide it down my throat via my nose but it's not going well. I am gagging and then there's more force. I taste blood. Finally it's in, I think. I don't know why they have to do this right now, haven't I suffered enough? Every part of my face and neck is screaming at me. Was I in a car accident? Did I have surgery for a head-on collision? This is so much worse than before. I hate that I am here, alone.

I try to be optimistic in the days that follow but I'm too tired. The nasal tube is torture and there's a plastic straw type thing in my throat, holding open an airway, something for the flap to grow around. I brought my iPad but I don't want to look at it. There's a drain in my leg this time and the incision is massive, running from above my knee all the way to the top of my leg. Walking to the bathroom is manageable but not easy—my left leg is weak and I am so tired. This surgery is worse in every way.

The nurse insists that I walk every day, which is embarrassing in this one-size-fits-all hospital gown. I look awful and feel feeble, my face is swollen and every direction I move my head is a new, painful discovery. I need to walk because in order to leave, I'll need to demonstrate that I am mobile. I try to sleep but every position is uncomfortable and they won't let me recline. They are tapering me off the high-powered pain meds and my sleep, the little glimpses I get, worsens. I am getting cranky, which isn't normally how I feel in a hospital setting. I am upset but unable to pinpoint why. Maybe it's the lack of sleep. Solid food is out of the question right now, they say. I haven't had anything food-like in my mouth in days, just ice chips. I want to be home so I can finally sleep and get past the sickly, stale feeling.

The nurses and assistants swap in and out, morning and night. I give myself a much-needed bath of sorts with hospital wipes. They are giving me something different to help with sleep, melatonin maybe. I manage an hour or two of calm escape. I'm waking up and something is happening with the wretched nasal feeding tube, this thing I hate worse than cancer. A nurse is standing over me and messing with it. I yell as best I can and turn my head even though it's unpleasant. "What are you doing? Stop!" I am furious—I want her out of my sight and reprimanded. My mouth is full with a half sirloin of leg muscle, a plastic straw is wedged into my swollen throat, along with a feeding tube that is also sutured to my nose. My ability to speak is impaired, and whatever I say is garbled and hard to follow but she seemed to get the message.

She apologizes, explaining something about the fucking nose tube, how it needed to be adjusted. *While I was asleep though?!* This makes me even angrier. *If you need to do something like that, wake me first. Say something to me, make sure I can understand what is happening. I am not in a coma. You can't just do this and hurt me—you have no idea what this feels like. My face is in so much distress and you just made it worse by poking around and now I just want to cry. Look what you did. I want to cry but I can't because I am too tired and tears take effort. I wish Dr. Barber was here. I wish someone was here, but it's just me, all alone in the hospital again.*

My walks get longer, one lap and then two, as I push my IV around nurses' stations and supply closets. No one seems to notice me or wonder why I'm out of my room. I hear people groan and scream, feeling grateful I'm no longer in that sort of pain. I will make it out of this place, soon, and see Lindsay again. I miss her, but we haven't really talked because my ability to speak and will to try is limited. I speak to the nurses and residents, even though I wish I didn't have to. My face and mouth are not my own now and I feel a deep sadness. But at least I can still walk.

I feel guilty about snapping at the nurse who messed with my nose tube. She didn't deserve that, her job is challenging and I don't want to be remembered as a difficult patient. *Before I go home, I will apologize.* The nose tube worked its way out—my body was not interested in more liquid nutrition. After nearly a week, I'm taking extended walks with less difficulty. My left leg is sore, but it can hold me. I am ready to be home. I will feel better when I can sleep in my own bed and wear normal clothes. I miss Lindsay but I'm glad she isn't seeing me like this, I wouldn't have been good company, all tired and ill-tempered. I apologize to the nurse for snapping. She looks confused at first, before thanking me, awkwardly, eyes pointed at the floor.

"Oh... well, okay. Thank you for that."

My stuff is packed up, leg bandaged as I walk to the bank of elevators; I've had so much practice walking, there is really no need for a wheelchair. Lindsay and I head home after I jokingly offer to do the southbound drive so she doesn't have to. The clutch would be tricky, but not impossible. I'm relieved to see the unmasked face of someone I know and love.

I spent less time resting than Lindsay would've liked. Being idle in bed was boring and I'd been lying down for the better part of a week, in the hospital, uncomfortable and grouchy. A few nights of uninterrupted sleep at home transformed me into someone motivated and ambitious.

Dr. Barber's instructions on recovery—how long I'd need to rest, limitations, etc—were, in my view, open-ended and subject to interpretation. I was not the sort of person who always followed strict guidance after surgeries, and I'd had so many of them that I could intuit when I'd had enough time "taking it easy." Still, I was not foolish, I would not go and do something crazy that could cause further injury. My leg was perfectly able to hold my weight but weakened; I would need some time off my bike. My face and mouth and neck were swollen, but healing. I'd already proved that my arm was capable of running my saws and working out in the shop.

I remembered the recovery from chemo and radiation, at the beginning, how it had taken a full year to recover from the damage. But I had recovered and I could again. I would be able to bike, to learn how to fly, but not for a while. I would need to heal and regain strength that had been lost from days in suspended animation, under anesthesia, from weeks in the hospital. I also needed a challenge, a sort of bespoke physical therapy. I knew exactly what I would do: remodel the bathroom.

Remodel

Lindsay and I had talked about updating our tiny bathroom —the only one in our modest house—since she'd moved in. The fixtures were dated, the tub too small, shower head too low. The space felt cramped, more closet than room, with a shower curtain dividing the area in half. Before the surgeries, I had mocked up a 3D design that would make better use of the limited space, swapping the tub for a shower with sliding glass doors and floor-to-ceiling tile. I've been home for a week or two. In the space of a month, I had two major reconstructive surgeries, each requiring week-long hospital stays and now I was ordering fixtures and supplies, writing out a project plan.

Lindsay informs me that taking on a project like this, right now, is unhinged. "You know this is crazy, right?" Lindsay looked at me as I turned around in my office, computer monitor behind me. I'd been comparing different types of sinks for the custom vanity I was planning on building. "You should focus on your recovery."

I smiled as best I could, eyes dancing with excitement for a New Big Project. "I am fine, honey. Dr. Barber even said she's amazed at how my leg is healing, the flap too." I was insistent. I had the time now and I wanted to prove I could still do something difficult and ambitious. Plus, I wanted to make our little house more pleasant to live in. We had always wanted a fancier bidet, and now we could have one, because I could do most of the work myself: demolition, framing, tile, fixtures, electrical.

I was ready to move and work. My body had been mostly immobile for so long and now I was home, but unable to speak like before. My left leg was weaker, but still worked, and my hands were unaffected. I was frustrated to have my face stuck in this state, voice hollow like speaking with a rubber ball sown to my cheek. *Is this what it's like for people who've had strokes?* I could only feel the left side of my jaw and moving my mouth required so much effort. I wasn't prepared for this. I had no idea it would be so difficult.

I refused to be depressed, to feel sorry for myself because that's not how I did things. Instead, I was going to pour all of that energy into the remodel. The old plaster walls were the first to go and I smashed them gleefully. I missed the old version of my face, the one that was more even. I felt like a chipmunk carrying around an acorn, but eventually the swelling went down. I needed to fix something, to see improvement. Healing wasn't happening fast enough. I wanted to feel capable because simple actions, like eating and talking, now required concentrated effort. My diet was soft foods, and I began to retrain my mouth to produce sounds. My leg was weak, too weak to bike but strong enough to get around. The bathroom project would be my way of deconstructing and rebuilding and the end result would be better than before, even if the same was not true for me.

The pandemic was still happening in the background. I went back to work but struggled. My escape, every day, was the remodel, the work I had control over, that didn't require so much verbal communication. I was my job and my voice and there was no separating the two. I wasn't loud or ostentatious (usually), but I could hold attention in a room or online meeting, and I treasured this ability. It wasn't something I'd always had, not in the context of work anyways. I'd been encouraged, pushed, to speak up and be more expressive. Coworkers—mostly older guys nearing retirement—helped me build confidence, mentoring me in those early years. Eventually, things began to click. I could lead a team in robust discussion, present to a large audience, facilitate meetings. It was thrilling, having my voice heard, being respected, looked to for guidance. How could I do any of that now, with a fucked-up mouth incapable of producing normal speech? The skill I'd been developing for so long, and the confidence I'd gained, was now breaking apart, just like the bony pieces of my palate. I didn't know how to grieve this loss, so I worked on the new bathroom.

Dr. Barber wanted the new flap to be fully healed before we resized it, so we spent another summer driving to Seattle for more hyperbaric treatments. This was not strictly necessary, but an extra measure to help ensure healing. As we were nearing the end of the hyperbaric treatments, around thirty-six of forty, Lindsay was informed that no one would be allowed in the waiting area due to a new hospital policy. We always drove together, like we had that day and she read books while I read mine in the submarine-like chamber. But now, because of new COVID precautions, this was not allowed. Lindsay sat in our parked car, cried, and texted me. After I changed out of my scrubs I told the front desk person that we were done—that was it—no more treatments. If Lindsay couldn't be here with me, what was the point? We were doing this together or not at all. The woman at the reception desk, a nurse, didn't seem surprised.

"I understand. Best of luck."

Thirty-six treatments was plenty. The flap healed and I had it reduced down. For six weeks, I would have another trumpet sown in place at the end of my nose—a rubber flange that held a straw-like tube, running from my nostril down into my throat. The idea was to create more airflow and space, for speech and swallowing, and force the flap to grow around it. I hated the straw and the trumpet was worse. I looked foolish and wearing a mask was painful. Speaking was already challenging and now we were adding a new hurdle.

I missed biking so we decided to get e-bikes, fancy ones with steel frames and German drivetrain components. In the past I had scoffed at people riding these battery powered bicycles. I called them mopeds and wondered why folks didn't get "real bikes" instead. And now, here I was, eating my words. *This will be the way I get back into cycling as I'm recovering,* I thought, *my leg can use the extra help.* An e-bike was not a paraglider, but feeling the air on my face at 30 mph, powering down hills, reminded me of the dream. I hadn't forgotten about flying. My copy of *The Art of Paragliding* sat in a prominent spot on the coffee table as a reminder. I would learn how to fly, life just needed to settle down first.

Of course, our lives did not settle, but the pandemic waned and people started doing things again—gathering together, getting married. I had said early on, just weeks into dating Lindsay, that marriage was a non-starter for me. And now I was about to change my mind. One night, over dinner, we talked about the idea of getting married. Our proposal was a discussion, romantic in its practicality. The topic had come up before; Lindsay worried about my end of life care, what might happen if we weren't married and Tim wasn't around.

The pandemic had tested so many relationships—we knew plenty of couples who did not last, who discovered that being in close proximity led to new forms of conflict, by unmasking traits and habits, or prompting challenges they hadn't weathered before. We realized the months in lockdown and the disruptive changes, in our daily lives, with my health, had strengthened our commitment. We had pivoted, adjusted, and enjoyed our time at home together.

Lindsay suggested we do something small with family and some friends, maybe at her family's farm. I listened and nodded.

"Ok, but what if, instead, we throw a huge party and invite everyone?" She rolled her eyes.

The simplest option was rarely the most fun where events were concerned.

"Alright, you get to plan it then."

A new project—I was thrilled.

Even as speaking was an ongoing challenge, relearning how to articulate, channeling breath into sound, planning was something I could do well in a reflexive sort of way. I liked breaking down an objective (have a big party, a wedding) into all of its constituent parts, categorizing them, putting dates and deadlines on tasks, thinking about budgets and vendors. There were so many moving parts, with a whiff of the unknown; we would be doing something completely unique and only once, and there would be friends and music and speeches. I was the architect and the planner, the person making choices, designing components large and small that, collectively, would add up to a memorable event. I couldn't do everything, of course, but I could shape the outcome.

We decided that the ideal location was the family farm, out towards Boston Harbor, so we reached out to Lindsay's dad and his wife. They loved the idea. We would wait another year, hopeful the pandemic would continue to fade, and then we would get married and celebrate.

The scars flattened and healed and my body was now adorned with the marks of a skilled craftsperson, wrist to elbow, knee to groin, ear to throat. The contrast between my left and right forearms gave me an idea—I would decorate the right one with a tattoo that reflected and celebrated the paddle-like scar on the left. I would add symmetry to my arms even if my face remained a touch askew. On my thirty-eighth birthday, I sat while another talented woman worked on my arm. The design was a fern, green and vibrant, growing out of a monotone crack, like one in pavement. Sitting for the tattoo reminded me of getting an IV. I would always watch and try to anticipate the discomfort of the needle, not alarmed, but curious. I watched Gina, the tattoo artist, trace outlines and geometric shapes in thick black lines, pressing firmly into my skin.

The thought of a forearm tattoo—anything plainly

visible in short sleeves—had been unthinkable before. Perhaps there was some strange, lingering idea of professionalism, that visible tattoos would make it harder to find a job. I had tattoos, one on my right shoulder and a more recent addition covering most of my right calf, but I had never given serious thought to a forearm piece. Perhaps a half sleeve, above the elbow, something hidden from view. The forearm scar changed my perspective. My left arm was already changed in a major way, modified surgically. The scars told the story and plenty of people asked. So why not change the corresponding arm, dress it up in color?

The flap surgeries changed my relationship with my body, mostly my face and mouth. I didn't really have a relationship with my skull base, because it wasn't something I gave any thought to, but after the drastic revisions and reconstructions, I imagined the deep recesses of my skull, what they looked like before, compared to now. Dr. Barber pointed out anatomical changes as she scrolled through an MRI. There was no symmetry between the left and the right and where bone once was, now empty space. I had a different face than before, all the way to the foundation.

For a while I was angry and frustrated because this new face, and mouth especially, didn't work like the old one. I was missing feeling and my jaw tired easily. The radiation had not only damaged the bony structures but also the connective tissues, making them brittle and inflexible. No treatment or medication could fix this, so I would need to stretch my jaw every day, cranking it open with the help of a special 3D printed device. If I stuck to this routine for life, my mouth would continue to open wide enough for eating and dental work.

The changes to my face would become my new reality,

what I lived with, not simply a one-time event like past surgeries or treatments. The way I spoke, the parts of my body
that enabled speech, were permanently altered. Speaking
had always been effortless and I'd built my identity around
it. And now it was labored, taking concentration to form
sounds with a throat and jaw that had been damaged
beyond repair and then rebuilt with borrowed pieces. I
remembered Dr. Barber telling me that things would
change. I'd made the decision because the alternative was to
suffer, to risk loss of life while in continual distress. We had
arrived at a place with no easy answers, just carefully
considered and painful tradeoffs. And now I was on the
other side of so many compounding decisions—able to
speak but not fluidly, able to eat, but not easily. There was so
much to adjust to.

What I could eat and how I ate it changed significantly,
and for several months after the surgeries, Dr. Barber
insisted I keep a food diary, documenting my caloric intake.
My new diet featured soft foods and protein shakes. I began
to learn the things I could swallow easily and the foods that
would cause a round of choking and regurgitation. I ate
ramen noodles and became very adept with chopsticks,
ideal for placing small, manageable bites of food in my
mouth. Almost everything I ate and tried to swallow would
require a glass of water—there was no such thing as 'inhal-
ing' a favorite food anymore. Eating would become a slow
and deliberate process, particularly for new and untested
foods.

Meals stopped being a social thing. Finding a restaurant
with foods I could comfortably eat was a process with layers
of trial and error. I avoided potlucks and gatherings where
food was the main feature. Eating had become a chore, a

necessary task. I didn't eat for fun or go out to brunch with friends because it was awkward and embarrassing. Explaining my limitations over and over again was tiring, but it was easy to forget the inside of my face was completely different, because the outside was mostly the same. There were few visible markers that told the story of being rebuilt in this way.

Speaking became easier as time went by. The pandemic ended and we rode e-bikes, sang karaoke, and finally enjoyed a summer without daily trips to Seattle. My speech had improved and I was less bothered by the change in diet —I bought a wok and a new cookbook and tried my hand at Asian dishes, soft foods with small, spicy bites. My relationship with food and eating would never be the same. My speech too, but I was still finding ways to experiment, learning new ways of doing things.

At some point in the long process of healing from two head/neck reconstructions, I started stretching. I called the routine of movements my stretches, but Lindsay would say "Yeah, that's yoga." I wasn't schooled in the art beyond a couple of classes, so stretches sounded more appropriate. My neck was different after all the work—being dissected twice changed things, sensations were blunted, movements limited. I didn't want to become stiff, so I started stretching my neck in these daily sessions. I would stretch my jaw too, and then massage the bony part on the right side, where the feeling was different. I thought about all of the trauma this part of my body had been through. My neck too, I appreciated it, knowing how much it had changed. I would stretch and focus my attention on these parts of my body that had been altered. Maybe this routine wasn't exactly yoga, but I was finding a way to sit with these new parts of myself, giving them compassion and care. I was grateful for medical science and modern reconstructive surgery, for the insurance that paid for it. And now I was working on building another sort of gratitude, for my body, the one I now possessed, with limits and new challenges.

Recurrence, Again

When my runny nose came back, I started joking that I probably had cancer again. My partner was not amused. "If you're going to joke about that, you need to see Dr. Barber and get new scans." Lindsay had acquired the bead business, which we had moved into our house. Nearly every wall in our home had pegboard, supporting thousands of beads and jewelry-making components. Lindsay and I had done this together in the space of a few weeks.

Finding the new baseline after two flap surgeries had been a slog, but we'd found ways to make my diet more interesting and eating was becoming less of a struggle. Dr. Barber was pleased with my progress, amazed even.

"You know, I tell my other patients about you, especially the ones who are struggling. Hearing your story, how you've come through this, it's really helpful for them."

I was touched that this world-class surgeon, someone I felt reverence for, held me in such high regard. I wasn't remarkable, I was just getting by and trying my best to laugh through the challenges. I was fortunate to know this woman, who spoke with candor and held my hand, reassuring me before life-altering surgeries.

I made an appointment and we were back in Seattle for scans, which Dr. Barber would review with us later that same day. After two years of being her patient, we finally saw her face. She walked into the exam room and Lindsay knew immediately.

"I'm so sorry," she said, sounding defeated.

This was not the outcome we wanted but it wasn't exactly surprising. We were at a second recurrence and the interval between them was becoming shorter. Three years had separated my diagnosis and the first recurrence and now barely two years had elapsed. Dr. Barber recommended that we chat with a friend of hers in oncology, about long-term options. Dr. Rodriguez was about Dr. Barber's age—my age—and she spoke plainly, without any cancer doctor jargon. She was thoughtful and kind, it was clear my prognosis bothered her. I imagined she was a dedicated provider; no wonder she and Dr. Barber were friends.

I already knew what she was about to tell me, that I had exhausted all of the treatment options. There would be another surgery but we were now playing a high stakes game of whack-a-mole. We would keep cutting out the cancer until that no longer made sense. We tried and exhausted all known treatments. The rareness of my cancer meant that clinical trials were uncommon, and if one did happen, it would probably require uprooting my life and relocating to a new city for a while, likely on the East Coast. I had no desire to start chasing cures in far away cities.

I thought about how all of this started—the early

promise of curative treatment, the confidence Dr. Vishnu that an aggressive regimen would give me the best chance. Even after the first recurrence, I was sure, utterly convinced, there was something we could do, some treatment that would allow me to beat the odds (unknown as they were) and be rid of this disease that kept barging in on my life. We went all in on proton treatment, and pointed more radiation at my face, which, in the end, didn't cure anything. More treatment had amplified my suffering, causing extensive damage that required drastic surgical repair. Now we were staring down another recurrence, maybe it was time to stop searching for something that did not exist and accept the reality: there is no cure.

I was not upset by the news; I breathed in deeply and started thinking, planning, wondering what we should do now that we were here again, dealing with cancer. This was not what we wanted, what we hoped for, but we did have the benefit of experience. So many years spent navigating treatments and side effects, diagnoses and medical subspecialties, surgeries and scans—Lindsay and I had become experts. The funny part was that I didn't have any other ongoing health concerns. None. My extensive medical history was centered around one condition, this rare and persistent thing.

My brother flew out after I told him. Over the years, we would speak often about my cancer journey. Tim understood, in a way others didn't, that I had accepted the idea that dying from this disease was a real possibility, an outcome that became more tangible, more likely, with every recurrence. He did not try to convince me otherwise or offer platitudes about cures.

"You never know what the cancer researchers might discover..."

"I'm rooting for you, your fight isn't over."

"No, no—Jonathan, you're going to live a long life."

This was something Tim understood intuitively, and his thoughtfulness as a brother and physician helped me navigate the frustrations and setbacks of dealing with cancer all through my thirties.

We talked enough about cancer and dying that when we spent time together, we liked to go on adventures. Tim was, since early childhood, a natural born adventurer. He would always find novel ways to explore the outdoors with me. Once, he bought a used tandem bicycle and we rode all around the Olympic peninsula, through Blyn and Sequim, from Shelton to Olympia, flying down the 101 in the highest gear. Our day at the hill in Boulder was a highlight and he knew about my dream, to learn how to fly paragliders. My surgery was scheduled, and in less than a week, the newest tumor would be removed. In the meantime, we would go flying. On a crisp day in October, we drove north and then east, to a suburban city outside of Seattle. Tim had booked us tandem flights at Tiger Mountain.

The barn-like building was cold and filled with paragliding gear. We signed waivers and sat in harnesses suspended from rafters. The atmosphere there can best be described as caustic bro energy. Between the crass jokes, the don't-tread-on-me flags, and the looped footage of tandem passengers vomiting, I felt uneasy and out of place. This was more of a boys' club than a business. But we were there to fly, that was the goal, and I could tolerate a bit of nonsense in the meantime.

Tim and I, along with a few other thrill seekers, piled

into a small bus, alongside the pilots we'd be flying with. One of them boasted about their club—it was the only place left where you could say gay as an insult. I was surprised, but the remark seemed on brand. We drove up the gravel road and I sat, listening to the chatter, not saying much.

People and gear were unloaded from the bus near the launch area. There were some clouds above us and the cold made my nose run even more. I would be flying with Frank and he took me through the basics of launch: keep running, even if we leave the ground for a moment, don't stop running. The flight was brief but longer than our solo flights in Boulder. We soared for ten minutes; the training flights in the park were a minute or less. As we flew, Frank let me take the controls and I turned the large wing, pulling the left toggle down, feeling the pressure and resistance. He asked if I liked rollercoasters—the answer is always yes—and we proceeded to perform movements I didn't know a paraglider was capable of, banking sharply, pulling g-forces. We landed in an open, grassy area near the barn.

Our flight in Boulder had been fun, but now I'd experienced a flight from a mountain. We soared over the tops of trees, above a forest, a few thousand feet off the ground. *These fabric aircraft can really maneuver. This is better than I'd imagined.*

I worked up the courage to ask someone about learning, but there were no clear answers. It sounded like there was some sort of apprentice program, but you had to get to know one of the pilots first. The website was no help—just information about flying tandem. *Oh well*, I thought, *this place was weird anyways.* The guy I'd flown with had been pleasant, but the vibe of the whole outfit was off. Whatever it was, it was not a place to learn how to fly. I would find an instructor and a school, maybe I would travel, but I would do it, after the surgery.

Thankfully, the procedure wasn't as complex or invasive as the flap surgeries. We blocked time off on calendars and got back to our day jobs. Lindsay was now working from home; the business was in the house, hanging from every wall. I had my office too, with the desk I'd built, and Lindsay and I would work and check in throughout the day. We texted frequently, separated by a hallway.

I spoke with Dr. Barber a few days later when she called me to discuss details about the surgery. I was concerned about my teeth and wanted to keep as many as possible. Dr. Barber said she would do her best, but there was a real chance all of the remaining top teeth, right canine to molars, would have to go. She explained that once I'd healed I would be able to get a prosthetic.

We were back in Seattle in the early morning and now that the pandemic had subsided, Lindsay could keep me company in pre-op. A large group of surgeons huddled near a table in the corner of my room. Dr. Barber saw Lindsay and walked over, opened her arms and hugged her. Dr. Barber explains to both of us that they won't really know the surgical approach needed until they open me up. There is some concern about the internal carotid artery, because the cancer has eaten away at some of the reconstructed tissue in that area. If it needs to be covered, they might take a bit of flesh from my hip.

All the teeth in question were sacrificed and I wake up, saddened as my tongue feels their absence. I learn later that Dr. Barber and her team were able to split and reattach part of my existing flap, making the surgery less invasive. In addition to my top teeth, they also took a bit of fat from my hip to help protect the artery in my face. I didn't realize I had any fat there. I am now a patchwork of additions and subtractions, a face thoroughly revised. The work to repair the damage from treatment did not change the trajectory of my disease. I still have cancer to contend with, an incurable variety that's fixated on the spaces behind my nose and eyes.

I'm now resolved to learn how to fly. It *will* happen the following year. But where? That was the big question now. Where am I going to learn and who is going to teach me? The place outside Seattle isn't a school and even if it was, no thanks. I want to feel at ease around my instructors, respected. This isn't the same as piloting a Cessna, but it's still significant, and there is real danger involved. I want to learn from someone competent at flying and skilled at teaching. I am under no illusion that one can teach themselves how to paraglide—proper instruction is a prerequisite.

I will need to plan this out, just as I need to plan the wedding. I send a note to my friend Katie from the YA cancer non-profit, explaining my dream of flying. She thinks learning to paraglide is a great idea and, as luck would have it, she knows a professional pilot. He could probably offer me some guidance on where to learn. This is real progress. I have a connection. I won't have to figure all of this out on my own. My mind is set on this goal, and that means it will happen because I am stubborn and single-minded when I fall in love with a new challenge. The bathroom remodel was a prelude to this—flying will be bigger and I will need more help. I cannot read books or watch videos and somehow learn to fly, I need someone to teach me.

Recovering from this surgery, where the latest tumor was removed, is easier than the cascade of reconstructive surgeries, like the difference between stitches and an amputation. But there is a new problem, one I feel guilty complaining about. I don't like to smile because I have a huge gap now, an empty space where the top right row of teeth used to be. I avoid pictures. Lindsay says I look cute but I don't, I look foolish. Eating changes a little because now chewing can only happen on one side. My speech sounds gummy, like a grandma without her dentures.

Dr. Barber examines my progress and gives me the sign-off to see the maxillofacial prosthodontist, Dr. Sutton. The dental offices are located on the same campus as the hospital, in a building that is connected by long corridors and banks of elevators. As you leave the hospital and get closer to the dental school, the vibe changes. The fixtures are dated, the lighting is worse, there are no names of donors on the walls, or contemporary art pieces. It felt like walking back in time, through a portal to a quieter place with fewer people moving about. I wondered how these places came to be connected, given how alien they were to each other in their appearance and character.

We arrive at the clinic and meet with Dr. Sutton. He had the laugh of someone who loved his work and made jokes about himself. All around us were pieces he helped create—fake noses and teeth, molds of mouths—displayed on countertops or behind glass. He explains the process of constructing me a device called an obturator. It will act like an artificial palate, filling in the open space left by the surgeries. I'll have a new row of teeth too, color-matched to my remaining ones. And this custom prosthetic will also be outfitted with something called a speech bulb, a piece affixed to the end of the obturator that will sit in the back of my mouth near my throat, preventing too much airflow, helping with speech and articulation.

Dr. Sutton tells me that the device will feel strange at first, but as I get accustomed to it, my obturator will become an extension of my own body. Molds are taken of my teeth and mouth and Dr. Sutton spends time in his lab on the weekend, crafting this bespoke prosthetic, adding wires that will hook onto my real teeth, securing in place the color matched artificial teeth that will complete my smile. We return to the dental clinic and he shows us his handiwork. It'll be fitted today, just a few minor adjustments and a rundown on how to care for it. It's removable, held in place by a a powdered version of the adhesive your grandma uses, with two thin wires that wrap around existing teeth.

I am excited to smile again, with a full set, without gaps. The bulb that sat further back in my throat felt odd, like it doesn't belong there and I might choke. Dr. Sutton assures me that in time this device will feel like an extension of my body. I am no longer hesitant to smile wide and express myself, to laugh wide open. I had been distraught about losing my teeth, disappointed to feel their absence when I woke from surgery, and now this part of me that I valued was restored. I didn't mind that it was artificial—it had been handcrafted by an artist, just for me, and I was proud and relieved.

I'd been living with my new prosthetic for a week when I decided it was time to talk to Nick, the paraglider pilot. My speech was better but I was still adjusting, learning how to form phrases with a mouth that had changed shape yet again.

I rang Nick, he was driving somewhere with spotty reception. I shared my tandem experience and he was sympathetic but not surprised. He knows the owner the boys' club, and they are problematic. He tells me the sport should be more inclusive, and is actively working to bring more women and minorities into paragliding. I'm encouraged; Nick seemed like a thoughtful guy.

"I am ready to dedicate serious time to learning. Paragliding's been a goal of mine for about ten years and Katie said you're the person to talk to."

I needed advice because I wasn't sure who to learn from. I'd read that finding the right instructor is one of the most important parts of becoming a pilot, so I wanted to be certain I was making the right choice. There was no way I could learn at the boys' club, and while I knew there were schools in Eastern Washington and in California, taking all of that time off work, coupled with living expenses, would be a challenge.

"You know, some good buddies of mine are instructors, they just started a school closer to you, at Tiger Mountain. Let me put you in touch with them."

Nick told me I would benefit from learning there, at Tiger, because everyone needed a home flying site and a community. I was overjoyed, knowing what needed to happen next, finally having an outline and people to talk to and learn from. I was eager to plan everything, to arrange my schedule and my life so I could focus my attention on becoming a competent and safe pilot.

I got in touch with a guy named Austin at Northwest Paragliding and soon I was poring over training checklists and the student agreement, which detailed baseline expectations for students during training. I was officially signed up to begin training for my P2 paragliding certification. We were still in spring, and flying season began in May, running through September. Austin explained that everything in paragliding was weather dependent, and often the most reliable conditions for learning were later in the season, August and September. I decided that's when I would start training. I would need to wait, but in the meantime, I had a wedding to plan.

The date was already set: mid-July. Save the date postcards had gone out and I designed actual invites and began working through items on my project plan. The venue was Lindsay's family farm and our budget was modest, so we only outsourced key roles—photography and catering. Everything else would be DIY. We planned on asking our friends and family members to donate to one of three funds instead of buying us stuff: a paragliding fund (for me), a Hawaiian vacation (Lindsay's dream), or a kitchen remodel (long overdue). I was hopeful that my family—my parents and godfather in particular—would make generous contributions.

Our wedding was lovely but hot with full summer sun. In my vows, I promise Lindsay we can finally get a dog. I smile wide in the photos, more confident now that I have my prosthetic. Despite years of cancer and treatment, surgery and recovery, I am still here, now married to my partner, this amazing woman who didn't leave when the cancer returned, early in our relationship. The post-ceremony speeches were a highlight. Listening to close friends and family describe how they saw us, as individuals, as a couple, was beautiful and humbling. My cancer came up several times because it was central to our story. Lindsay had been with me from early in the journey, our relationship was shaped and tested by hardships, experiences that most couples might have later in life, after decades together. Tim spoke and said that I suffered well. Listening to Tim and others describe how they saw me, and Lindsay, was illuminating. I was beginning to understand resilience, from another perspective.

The dream was so close, learning to fly, becoming a paraglider pilot. But there was a problem—we couldn't afford it. We hadn't raised nearly enough money. I had hoped for a level of generosity from my family that felt reasonable to me, knowing how long I'd been dealing with cancer, how little I'd asked for in the past. I wanted them to acknowledge me by helping, by giving me something tangible. They gave nothing. The sting of disappointment turned into anger—at them, at myself.

Maybe this was poor planning—what was I thinking pushing for a big event? We could have done something smaller and less costly like Lindsay's sister. My optimism extended in all directions and I wanted so badly for my parents to help in some small way. I wanted a gesture of generosity that was unusual for them, something that could be quantified. I was grateful they'd traveled here, to be a part of our wedding, to see a ceremony that was fully secular and thoughtful and full of love. I wanted them to have a view into our lives, a picture of who I was, with Lindsay and so many others we cared about. This day was exceptional, we were too, and I wanted to feel deserving of a gift.

I started to consider the possibility of financing or fundraising, but I was running out of time. I would need to start training in a month and there were no ideal options. Maybe I should just wait longer, be more patient. I'd waited ten years already, what's another year or two more? That would give us more time to save up. Hopefully I wouldn't get cancer again, but there were no guarantees there. If I tried to fundraise, did I know anyone that hadn't already given us a cash gift, or donated to the paragliding fund we'd set up on our wedding site? How could I ask these folks for more money, when my own family members weren't willing to give? And this was by definition a luxury thing, a privilege. I felt guilty and disappointed now. Maybe my dream was too much and I should just give up.

Tiger Mountain

Lindsay knew what flying meant to me and she wasn't about to let it go. She became single-minded and focused, like I'd been remodeling the bathroom. She called an old friend and explained our situation, the dream I'd had for so long and the opportunity to finally reach it, to learn how to fly at Tiger Mountain. Without a second thought, this friend offered to cover the entire cost of the gear I'd need. I was floored. The problem was solved, just like that, with sheer generosity. Lindsay wasn't too proud to ask for help, she knew people cared about us, about me and this crazy flying dream. I was deeply grateful and I would carry that feeling into my training and my flying. This was finally going to happen, despite all of the setbacks and disappointments. I was going to learn how to fly.

Fortunately, I had a job and a manager who knew about my cancer and my flying dreams. Working part-time during training wouldn't be a problem. I was grateful to have grown a career at an organization that gave me this sort of flexibility and I was beginning to recognize that I deserved it.

Work was important, but so was dedicating time to my dream. A YA cancer non-profit helped too, awarding me a grant that covered part of the training program fees. I agreed to write a piece about the experience they would share online.

Now that I had the schedule, the gear, and the money parts sorted, there was one final challenge: getting to Issaquah from Olympia. The commute, in usual traffic, was about 1.5 hours each way, which would be difficult to do multiple times a week. Lindsay and I had done a version of this—twice—for hyperbaric treatment. Thankfully, I managed to work out an arrangement to stay with a group of pilots and instructors in Issaquah on my off work days.

I wasn't sure what to expect—with training, the people I'd be living with. I was out of my element, away from home and my usual routines, but I resolved to be open-minded and grateful. I met the tandem pilot who would become my roommate—a middle-aged Brazilian dude named Indy, who was warm and outspoken. The house reminded me of the duplex with rented rooms and frequent guests, shared meals and mismatched dishware.

The stories I heard of how people got into the sport seemed improbable: an engineer who walked away from a lucrative career, a foreigner who got lucky at the casino one night and then let a buddy talk him into buying a glider, a cattle rancher turned pilot. Most of my instructors were also competitors—highly accomplished pilots who had set records and flown all over the globe. They lived in Sprinter vans and traveled, led tours and coached new and seasoned pilots alike. I admired this level of commitment but didn't know what inspired it. I was there to learn, to absorb all of the knowledge and advice I could, to immerse myself in paragliding and become a pilot.

Before new students got into the air on their own, there were some hurdles to clear, necessary steps to ensure interest, physical and mental ability. In addition to extensive practice handling a wing on the ground, everyone would need to fly tandem with an instructor, early in training, and then later on before you were cleared to fly solo. Learning at Tiger Mountain was not like the hill in Boulder, where we launched and flew on our own after just a few hours of training. Places like Boulder—with gently sloping hills, wide open space, few obstacles—allow for a different sort of training approach, where students can very quickly get in the air, taking many brief flights in a single day, walking back up the hill, flying down, over and over.

This experience would be different because Tiger is not exactly a beginner site; there is no training hill. There were hazards—a forest of trees below you, power lines, other pilots—and navigating them required awareness. Getting to launch—situated at 1,800' above the ground—requires an hour-long hike or shuttle ride up a forest road. The landing zone, or LZ, is a grassy area the size of a football field, which is near a trailhead. Around it—trees, a walkway, and a parking lot. The margin for error here was narrower than a wide open field or gentle hillside.

The first checklist item for the new paragliding trainee: two introductory tandem flights with one of the instructors. This was different from the tandem with Frank, because this time I was being evaluated. Our team of instructors needed to be sure we actually wanted to learn how to fly, could focus while airborne, and follow instructions. Learning required real effort and there were risks—a prospective student needed to be serious, willing to dedicate the time and respect the process. And just because you wanted to fly didn't guarantee you could.

My tandems were uneventful. The launches were better than the one with Frank and I listened and learned about the landing considerations and the normal pattern used. I spent more time controlling the glider than before, which seemed easy. I pulled the control and the glider changed direction. My instructors also showed me how to lean into a turn using my body weight, making it more efficient. After the in-flight mini-lessons, I was absolutely convinced. I was going to learn and be a fantastic student.

With no red flags on my tandem flights, I was cleared to begin training. I would start working to develop the skills I'd need to become a competent and safe beginner pilot. The schedule was weather dependent. Unlike classroom learning, we couldn't map out practice sessions months, weeks, or even days in advance. Everything depended on the wind. I quickly learned that long range forecasts were more like concepts, suggestions of what might occur, but never accurate enough to make concrete plans around. Not until about twelve hours beforehand, anyways.

I hadn't structured my schedule in such a free-form, last-minute way since my twenties. But the natural environment couldn't be project managed. We would need to conform, and build our decisions around its behavior. In practice, this meant updates in a group thread around 9 pm, when the latest wind and weather models were updated. Based on the wind strength and direction, the instructors would make a call on where and when the upcoming day's training session would take place. The message goes out, the students are tallied, and then it's time to rest.

I helped load the student kits into vehicles each morning on training days, lifting beanbag-sized sacks overhead, stuffing them between rows of seats. The wind was set to be ideal for a day of training. There wouldn't be any flying though—me and a half-dozen other students would be practicing with our gliders on the ground, a discipline known as kiting. The general idea is that you simulate the movements performed at launch, landing and flying while on the ground, building muscle memory to repeat those actions, allowing your glider to become an extension of yourself. I knew nothing about handling a glider beyond what I'd seen on YouTube and observed on my tandem fights. We arrived at a park with a dusty field next to a baseball diamond. It was hot, but not yet oppressive. Before we started practicing, there were some basic rules: helmets on, brakes in hand, always be prepared to be lifted unexpectedly and react quickly. When there is wind, the glider will want to fly and our task is to control it, to harness the latent energy and move in concert with our fabric aircraft.

We spent several hours practicing inflations and launch techniques. Everyone was a newbie like me. I watched my instructor, mystified at how he controlled his glider so effortlessly, holding the controls, knowing when to provide the right input, where to move and lean. All of it felt counterintuitive, like trying to write a sentence backwards with your non-dominant hand. By the end of the first day's training, I am sweaty and dusty and ready for a cold beer.

Our kiting sessions rotate to different locations depending on the projected wind. We practiced forward launches in low or nil wind in the Tiger LZ, where you run and use the momentum and force of your body to help inflate the glider. In vast, open fields near Mount Si, with steady winds, we could work on reverse launches—facing the glider, strategically pulling the risers and allowing the wind to fill the canopy and stabilize overhead as you maintain control and prepare to turn and face forward. I was learning how to inflate and turn—always left—in preparation for launch, how to disable the wing if I need to abort a lunch attempt, where my hands need to go, and how to propel myself forward with the glider above. We continued to practice in the summer sun, taking frequent water breaks in the shade of a parked car or nearby tree. Our instructors have battery-powered skateboards and they zip across the field, assisting students, shouting out guidance while wings are overhead, dancing. "Left hand up, left hand up. Good! Now keep running."

After a full day of practice, we usually make our way to the LZ so I can observe more advanced students completing their training flights. A beginner pilot needs thirty-five successful flights and a passing score on a written exam to earn the P2 certification. The governing body of paragliding and hang gliding, USHPA, refers to this milestone as a *license to learn*, emphasizing the slow and deliberate progression of skills needed to fly safely.

After several practice sessions, I realized that I was not a natural, that learning how to manage this aircraft on the ground was going to be difficult and strenuous. Learning to fly was going to be a slow process. I had waited for so many years, to get here, to learn how to fly, and I would. I was learning that patience was a fundamental part of this type of flying, and I felt supported by my instructors and confident in myself that I would get there.

Some days I would go up to launch and observe, watching other students ready their gliders, standing on fraying astroturf, looking lost and overwhelmed. One of our instructors is usually standing out in front of them, observing the wind, radio in hand. Every student who has gotten to this point, early in their sequence of thirty-five flights, has a radio strapped to their harness; they will receive guidance from our instructors while flying, one instructor ensuring they launch and fly away from the mountain successfully, another on the ground, taking over once they come into view.

The launch and landings are critical, and also where most incidents occur. Flying, by comparison, was the easy part. Every site has its own characteristics, but at Tiger, the steep incline at launch, the surrounding canopy of trees meant that launching required attention and care—to the wind, trees, other pilots. Misjudging or overcorrecting could easily mean a broken leg or treetop rescue. And when a flight comes to an end, your landing gear are your legs and feet. Sprains and breaks from stumbles and poorly timed landings happened, along with low altitude encounters with trees and thorny bushes.

The summer days are long and students fly until just before sunset, when the light begins to dim as the westerly face of Squak Mountain casts its shadow on the LZ. The air is calmer this time of day, like the mornings, which is ideal for student flights. The turbulent and thermic mid-day air is a different reality, one we have not experienced yet.

Spending time in the LZ sitting and observing, you are likely to make new friends. The excitement of pilots landing always attracts attention here. I met another student, Hakan. We shared the outlines of why we'd decided to do this improbable thing, learning how to fly while nearly forty. I told him the abridged version of my cancer tale and Hakan talked about a malaise he was trying to shake, something he hoped a new hobby might cure. I got the sense he was angry and I wondered why. I was certain, right then, that Hakan and I would be friends. Over lunch, he told me his story— leaving Turkey, coming to the US with his wife, being successful in his career but feeling disillusioned with the world, the constant striving and materialism. We were both looking for something, in the sky and within ourselves.

Our training schedule continued and I started to get better, slowly. Once I demonstrated consistency with controlling the glider, keeping it overhead and stable, inflating and deflating it with relative ease, then, and only then, would I be cleared to proceed to the next step: the simulated solo. This is the final check before I can fly solo and sail off the mountain under my own wing. The setup is like a tandem, in that I would be attached to my instructor. But they would not be doing most of the flying—I would, while listening to another instructor on the ground. I was being tested again. Could I follow commands while piloting this lightweight, unpowered aircraft?

We launched the tandem wing and my instructor handed me the controls. I flew away from the hill, heading straight towards a lake that's miles away, northwest of us, glassy blue.

"Ok, let's go ahead and make a right turn now. Right turn," my instructor on the ground says.

I pull the right brake and the glider begins to turn slowly, with a wide berth like a hefty sea vessel. Next, a left turn. Slow and steady. I'm told to head back towards the LZ, which I can see below me. My instructor takes back the controls and we land. I've passed. After three weeks of kiting practice on solid ground, I am ready to fly on my own.

We drove up to launch in a trail-worn van with our student gliders and my hands are nervous and sweaty. Mentally, I feel prepared, ready to follow instructions, confident that I can be attentive and make the right decisions—but my body is telling me something else, it's already reacting. It's late afternoon and the wind is calm, perfect for training flights. As we unload, I run through checklist items, doing mental pre-flight preparation. I notice my heart rate is up, mouth dry. *I have trained for this. Deep breaths.* The glider is carefully laid out in preparation for a forward launch where I will run, using my momentum and body weight to inflate the wing, and then continue moving forward until I am in the air, flying away from the mountain. "Radio check Jonathan." My instructor alerts the other instructor on the ground that I'm up next, on a red and yellow student wing. There are cameras pointed at me, other students capturing my first solo flight and bystanders who are amazed that anyone would do this. I'm in launch ready position, arms out, controls in my hands with lines draped over my forearms, faded blue and red on top of the dull pink scar and green fern.

This was like Boulder except that I am on a mountain, not a training hill.

"Whenever you're ready," says my instructor.

More deep breaths. I'm glad I learned how to meditate. I ran forward and the wing catches the air, slowly rising behind me. I can't see it but I can feel it. My shoulders are forward and I keep the pressure until I feel a bright stabbing in my left shoulder—it's trying to dislocate itself, I know this feeling. Years ago, I'd fallen off my bike and my shoulder had never been the same, popping out every so often at inopportune times. The glider is now overhead and I bring my arms down so I can run, and the shoulder pops back to where it belongs. It will hurt tomorrow but I am fine. *Just run.* I'm on a slope so there aren't many steps until I am in the air, suspended under my wing, flying.

Now it's time to listen and pay attention and fly predictably and safely. I complete the turns as instructed. I see the LZ and make note of my height above the ground. More turns, some 90 degree, some 180. The LZ is closer now. I have no idea how much time has passed because I am in a state of hyper focus—I want to fly well. I've seen this go wrong because of inattention and bad decision making; just last week a new pilot crashed into a treetop turning into the LZ and fell twenty feet. I will not be that student. I begin the setup for landing and the trees feel so close to my feet, too close. One more turn and then I'm coming in for the final approach.

"Ready... and flare, hands all the way down."

I slide in on my ass, just like in Boulder. Hakan is there and we celebrate the achievement.

The radio guidance on those early flights is a set of training wheels. Not much decision making is needed, just common sense. "If I say 'turn left' and there's a tree there, don't fly into the tree." Each flight in the journey to thirty-five is a milestone, and we take turns filming the launches and landings of other students, sharing them in our group chat. We are so excited for each other, recounting details of recent flights as we bounce around in the van. We are pioneers, pilots in the making. All of this is remarkable and we did it, after so many hours sweating in the sun, kiting our hearts out. We know so much more than before and every flight is another step towards greatness.

Around flight number twenty-five, I'm cleared to fly my

own wing. I won't be needing the tank-like student rig anymore. I've been kiting my brand new blue and orange glider for a while, so I know how to inflate and set up for launch, I just haven't christened it in the summer airspace yet. My shoulder is fine but I've decided to switch to a reverse launch just to be safe. This technique puts less strain on the shoulders, but requires waiting for the right little bit of wind, and then moving backwards and pulling up, almost like reeling in a big fish, allowing the wing to come over-head, and then turning, running, and launching, all in a single, fluid motion. It's balletic, when executed well. I wait, inflate, turn, and launch. I am flying my own wing, a wedding gift from a generous friend. My glider handles differently, it's more nimble and responsive to my inputs. I am going to know this wing as I've known my bikes, the ones I rode for thousands of miles. But I will treat it better than a steel road bike. I will take care of it. I fly from north launch in silky smooth air on an evening in September and look out towards Lake Sammamish as the sun is setting in the distance. I turn carefully, making sure I have plenty of altitude, as I head back towards the LZ. I land on my feet and we all celebrate. My glider is so new and bright and now it's been flown.

The radio isn't as important closer to thirty-five flights, less training wheels and more security blanket. Thirty-five flights is an arbitrary number, but by this time I've shown competence with launching and landing, in mostly calm conditions, and I've managed to do some ridge soaring, using warm, rising air flowing up the sides of the mountain to fly longer, moving along the ridgeline and then back again. I take the test and pass on the second attempt.

After years of dreaming, I've learned how to fly. I was

brand new, just beginning to gain understanding of the types of flying I was not qualified to do—flying in thermic conditions, flying at sites with more involved launches and landings, flying in strong wind. My range was narrow but I was eager to do more, to fly in more places, add hours to my log book, to be a safe and measured pilot who other people enjoyed sharing the sky with.

The training pushed me and I didn't progress as fast as the younger folks who ran every day or climbed mountains. The reality was, I couldn't move at that pace anymore; I needed to slow down. At home and at work I wanted to move quickly, to learn and build and accomplish, in a constant frenzy of activity. If I could just do more in the same amount of time, then I'd be making progress towards what I really wanted. The hospital stays and the adjustments after reconstructive surgeries, accepting myself in this altered state—none of it happened quickly, but I'd wished that it had. I was impatient, in need of something that would take hold of my attention, distracting me from uncomfortable truths about how I'd changed.

Physically, I would never be the same. I'd lost something, an energy that would allow me to snap back, a fully functional jaw, the ability to have a normal diet. In my thirties, even after treatments and tumor removals, I would recover and settle back into a body that was familiar. Now, permanently changed, I was pushing up against new limits, while figuring out what they were. I was proud to have finally learned the basics of flying a paraglider. I didn't know much —but I was aware of that—and I'd been patient with myself, more patient than I usually was in other areas of life. Slowly, I'd built the muscle memory to launch and land, and I'd learned to see distances and read the wind in new ways. I remembered checklists and safety considerations, and could recognize when I was out of my depth and shouldn't fly.

I was learning to be more patient because in paragliding, waiting is fundamental. In time, I would take longer flights, fly higher, fly in new places. I would push myself, just enough to make progress, within reasonable limits for me. There would be new challenges, and mostly, they would be the product of my mind.

Progression

There are a wide variety of people who take up paragliding. Engineers and software developers are overrepresented in my community at Tiger, but ages run from nearly teenage to very retired and we all get along pretty well. Our graduating class of newly minted P2 pilots included a mix of young-sporty-outdoorsy types, middle-aged dads who needed a new hobby, and people like me and Hakan, who were adventurous, but in a more measured, forty-year-old sort of way. We were both in decent shape, but we didn't build our lives around fitness or self-optimization. We liked books and ideas. Our work and hobbies reflected this, both centered around solving interesting problems. We were the bookish, nerdy, middle-aged pilot types, with no kids and broad interests.

Hakan and I were hungry to fly in new places after becoming certified newbies at Tiger. We wanted to explore, but not too far, fly, but not for too long. Our flying style was conservative—we weren't going to take outsized risks or push up against the limits of our skill; that was a young man's game, one that might land you in a tree or scraped up on a rocky hillside. We admired the younger guys who were more talented, who had the chops to do maneuvers we'd seen our instructors or seasoned pilots do. We were aware of our own limitations and this knowing gave us a different sort of camaraderie.

We took a trip to central WA, meeting a handful of other new pilots near Saddle Mountain. I'd been researching all of the beginner-friendly flying sites in WA and OR, and the goal was to fly as many as I could. I built a custom Google Earth file with ten different sites pinned, complete with links to site guides and reference materials. Saddle Mountain, the part people would fly, faces south, with a long bare ridge rising from the cracked desert. The area around it is pitted with tracks from dirt bikes and ATVs—a playground for big trucks with knobby tires. The road up to launch is less of a road and more a sandy suggestion that people have taken. We arrive at the top of the mountain, greeted by vicious wind and cold. There is a knowing look between Hakan and me, and the gliders stay in the car. We are not flying in these conditions.

Two of our friends are there—brothers—both talented and more tolerant of cold than me and Hakan. Another friend too, a pilot we learned with at Tiger, with roughly the same degree of skill and experience. He is determined to fly today. The wind is whipping, screaming up the ridge, into our faces. I have on all of my clothes and occasionally Hakan and I hop back in the car to defrost. Our determined friend is not skilled with high wind launches—he's never done them—but he resolves to change that today. Before the wing can rise overhead, he is dragged back, dragged twenty or thirty feet across the rocky ground. He tries again, this time with us bracing the glider, so he can bring it up without being dragged backwards. Another near miss. I'm envisioning a concussion or broken ankle if this continues.

Hakan and I try to reason with him. "Maybe you should call it good for today, we don't want you to get hurt." There was a reason neither of us were attempting this stunt, but his mind was made up. "I just really want to fly today," he says. The wind in our location is now close to the flying speed of our gliders, something we call trim speed. This means that if our headstrong friend manages to get airborne, he will need to immediately engage his speedbar, allowing him to fly a bit faster than trim speed, moving into the wind and away from the mountain. If he doesn't, he is going to be blown back behind launch, which would likely result in a painful crash against rocky ground. This is an advanced maneuver on a good day and I can hear one of my instructors admonishing him for taking this sort of risk.

We stand behind his glider again and the wind has filled it in an instant. I'm picturing all of the ways this might go wrong, annoyed he didn't just give up. We were supposed to have an adventure today, but now I am imagining an emergency crew shepherding our friend into the back of an ambulance. I'm glad I am not his age anymore and so fucking reckless. Through some uncanny luck, he manages to control the glider long enough to bring it overhead and is instantly plucked thirty, forty, fifty feet into the air. He's doing something like hovering, not moving forward and engages the speedbar, inching slowly away from the hill, towards the ridge where the wind is less compressed. Hakan shakes his head and we drive down the mountain, back over the mountain pass, towards home. Our friend flew for over an hour and landed near his car, parked on the wide open flatland below the mountain.

I was new to paragliding but learned that the want to fly is only one consideration of many. This sport is often waiting, not flying, for a variety of reasons. The wind is too weak or too strong, maybe coming from the wrong direction. The clouds might be too low or the sun not yet bright enough to create the lift you want. Patience is fundamental.

The idea of doing something more than cautiously flying and landing in a pre-determined location is still far afield. I am aware of other disciplines within the sport— speed wings that buzz over treetops, doing high-speed barrel rolls, and acro pilots performing stomach wrenching, high-G maneuvers at higher altitudes. Neither interest me. Speedflying seems needlessly reckless and designed for the GoPro adrenaline set and acro would destroy my shoulders. There is a third type of flying, one that my instructors have talked about, which involves gaining altitude and traveling real distances—cross country (XC) paragliding. Skilled pilots on ideal weather days have travelled significant distances—hundreds of kilometers—traversing mountain ranges, flying over desert and forest, along coastlines. I was amazed by the people I knew who did this sort of flying, the planning and stamina involved. I had found the next step: building the skills to take a cross country flight.

Before I could go cross country, I would need to learn how to climb and gain altitude instead of slowly losing it on a leisurely sort of flight that we call a sledder, as in sledding down a snowy hill. You go up top, you sled to the bottom. By now I've flown in a variety of places, in mild to moderate conditions, and my longest flights have been sustained by ridge light, wind that hits the face of a cliff or mountain side and is channeled upwards, forming a playground for soaring.

Hakan and I drove out to Fort Ebey in the spring, joining more seasoned pilots, waiting around in the park, all of us hoping the forecasted wind will materialize. Finally it does and we launch, nervously moving forward towards the cliff's edge. In seconds we are soaring above the Pacific coast. We fly down along the ridge line and back again, just a few hundred feet above the ground, past the nest of a bald eagle. We spend an hour that felt like a day soaring back and forth with other pilots.

Learning how to inflate my wing, to launch and land safely was a challenge, a milestone I needed to pass and then, I reasoned, I would be comfortable flying, able to sail effortlessly, accumulating hours and skills by virtue of doing it over and over again. I would learn actively, on my own, much like I had learned to be a proficient cyclist. But I'd been mistaken. None of it was easy anymore, I was on my own, without the security of my radio and instructors nearby. I flew with friends, sure, but up in the air I was alone with myself, fully responsible for what happened. The hyper focus was still there, but now it was restricting—I was still in training mode, lacking the capacity to do anything else. I would need to resolve this if I was ever going to try flying cross country. That sort of flying required a new level of decision making and planning, plus I needed to learn how to tolerate, even enjoy, the often bumpy, rising air. If I was going to do XC, I needed to learn how to thermal, and to do that, I would need to relax.

By nature, I am not much of a worrier. My life before cancer was relatively worry-free and I moved through most days with a steady sort of optimism. The worst thing had already happened, and I got through it well enough, so by comparison whatever trouble or setbacks I might face from then on were not worth the worry. I didn't worry in life but increasingly I did worry in the sky, while flying. *What if my obturator falls out and is lost to the forest? What if another pilot flies too close and I have to make an evasive turn?*

The whole reason I'd taken up flying, why I'd been dreaming about it for so long, was the lightness and freedom I'd felt under a canopy. It was fun. I felt alive and joyful and I wanted more. But now I was worrying and tense —I was experiencing more stress than enjoyment, carrying tension in my hands and back. Holding the controls, I gripped so tight that my fingers would go numb after a while. I never felt particularly comfortable in the harness even though I knew it was adjusted properly. When I hit some rough air, I would tense up, like I was trying to do sit-ups in the sky. The nerves were beginning to impact the joy I'd felt when I first started flying. I wasn't having fun. And sometimes the flight would be enjoyable, at first, and then the ache of worry would seep in.

I felt stuck, like I wasn't progressing, just a perpetual newbie. One day at Tiger, I was flying mid-day, trying to work up the nerve to take a longer flight, to find lift and stay in it. My wing would catch hints of a thermal, the turbulent edges that often surrounded stronger lift, and instead of turning into it, I panicked and flew the opposite direction, towards calmer air. I went and landed safely and my instructor looked at me, after glancing up at pilots who were still flying.

"Were you trying to come in and land?"

Yes, I was, because I was afraid.

There was something missing, confidence maybe, and in

its absence was more worry. I did not expect paragliding to be this difficult, taxing on my psyche like a fraught romance. Flying looked effortless, the videos I'd seen early on, the ways my instructors and friends flew and talked about flying. That's what I wanted—to relax and do new things while still having fun.

Learning by doing was usually my approach, but I was going to need hands-on instruction to become a better pilot. I was not a natural like some of the folks I learned with, mostly younger guys, fit and daring and ambitious. All of the surgical alterations had changed me in profound ways, I felt like I'd aged a decade. My body was not the same and I was still learning to love and accept it. I knew I would progress, but it would just take longer.

My buddy Seth had also been a worrier when we met, early in my training; he didn't seem to be enjoying flying very much. I was too new to diagnose what he was going through, but now it seems like he was probably stuck in a similar way—unable to relax enough to try new things and take the calculated risks needed to progress. Eventually Seth worked through this in-flight anxiety and became a well-rounded and highly competent pilot. He flew more, built trust in himself and his skills, and found challenges that suited his risk tolerance—not too much or too quickly—and over time the fear became manageable. He even started working on a tandem rating that would allow him to take others flying. One of the requirements to obtain this endorsement involves completing thirty-five tandem flights, but only with other licensed pilots. Seth asked if I wanted to fly with him and the answer was: "Yes, of course!"

Seth might have been a worrier in the sky because he is a worrier in general. Perhaps this is a product of his upbringing or career as a first responder. In a group of people, Seth would be the one most concerned about the rules being followed. He was serious about most things, including having fun, and he didn't like people messing with his stuff. His humor was often so dry it would be hard to know if he was joking or admonishing. Seth, like most people who throw their lives into this sport, was a bit eccentric. He was also exactly the sort of person you wanted around when something crazy happened. If a student flew into a tree, he would be coordinating the rescue effort.

Seth and I got set up to launch in the usual way— unpacking the glider, checking the lines and harness, donning helmets and leg straps. His tandem wing was new to him, purchased from another pilot, red and white and sturdy looking. Another part of the tandem training involves a mandatory briefing, like that one I got from Frank years back, and Seth delivers it to me. It was a late summer day and we launched in mild wind from the north. Throughout our flight, he narrated his actions and decision making. We fly into some lift and then out the other side and circle back, trying to find it again. Seth is calm and he doesn't seem worried. He notes the other pilots, reminding himself and me that we have company. I see the faces of people I know fly by. We follow another pilot who has found some lift, and is now at a higher altitude than us. There's a little climb but nothing exceptional. Seth is flying this glider with a sense of ease and I am there with him, relaxed. I'm holding on, but not too tightly. We soar the ridge for a while and set up for an easy landing. We've flown for nearly an hour and I am refreshed and ready for more.

The fear and worry didn't go away instantly but a half

dozen tandems, with Seth and others pilots I knew, helped reset something in my first season of flying.

Seth was more cautious than other pilots and I could hear the outlines of his thought process in fight. Maybe I was reassured that he had gotten better, like I wanted to, that his worry was still there, but more measured. Flying tandem with Seth and other more experienced pilots helped me learn, through observation. Trying on my own simply wasn't enough, I needed to be shown, mentored. My instructors were mentors too, but whatever worries they had were generally wrapped up in the mechanics of running a small business while guiding students through activities that carried significant risks. In flying they had already progressed so far that it was hard to relate, to imagine them as new pilots. Their advice was always helpful but their struggles were different.

As the flying season began to wind down in the fall, when the weather turned to dark shadow cloud and rain, I realized I now had a new perspective, a way of moving through discomfort. I could see it as information rather than distress signals, and greet it with more curiosity and less fear. I'd already learned lessons like this about pain, through all of the treatments and surgeries, especially the more recent ones, where I'd been reconstructed.

I was determined to continue progressing and shed some of the worry so I could fly longer, and hopefully someday complete a cross country flight. I needed mentorship and training, to be around skilled pilots who could help guide me in overcoming my fear and give me tips on planning. I was ready to take the next step and dedicate some time to this endeavor, having recovered from flap surgeries, the revision, and the most recent cancer surgery. We still saw Dr. Barber for scans every so often, but we were approaching the threshold where the drives to Seattle would become less frequent.

I thought about recurrence, but it was less of a worry and more of a fact, something that would happen eventually. After years and years of living with the reality of a cancer diagnosis that evolved into a recurrent, incurable condition, I'd adopted a matter-of-factness in how I thought and spoke about it. There would always be a landscape of unknowns, but I could make reasonable best guesses about where all of this was headed. And given the intractable nature of the rare cancer I had, future recurrences seemed abundantly more likely than a miracle moment where— absent any treatment or intervention—the cancer vanished. After two recurrences, I was resigned to the idea that there would be more in my future.

I was not fearful of this outcome; I could plan around it, it was a challenge to be solved. Maybe the cancer couldn't be cured, but I could still live an exciting and fulfilling life, and I would do that by being honest about the reality of my disease. In my flying, I did not have the same depth of understanding. I did not know the wind or the sky, the geography, my wing in this intuitive way. I had not been through a broad range of experiences with these elements, as I had with my own body, during my cancer journey. Even my own reactions surprised me, when I encountered unexpected situations in the sky. I was fearful—that I wouldn't be able to plan, to react in a measured way. I did not want to make foolish mistakes, to overcompensate or misjudge, and embarrass myself or my instructors. And maybe I was also afraid of injury, something that would cost me the ability to fly, which could be game over—no more flying, done forever.

Recurrence #3

The year was new, nearing spring, and the runny nose was back. The time in remission was even shorter than before— three-and-a-half years, then two-ish, and now barely a year. The last recurrence had galvanized me to finally learn how to fly. I had gone part-time at work and directed all of my focus to the effort. My dream of flying had been realized and I could soar, competently and safely. I was starting to over- come fears and improve, but I needed to fly more often.

My priorities needed to be reshuffled. I'd reached a plateau in my career and while I was usually content, I would oscillate, every year or so, between feelings of boredom and disillusionment, eager for change, but also reticent, uncertain what I could or should do. I felt stuck. I'd promised myself early on that I would not dissolve my sense of self, my identity, into my work. And in those early years, I didn't—there was space between me and my job. But as time wore on, I wondered if I had made a public sector version of the same mistake I'd made at the internet company, only in slow motion, building my identity around the mission and the work, over years instead of months. My job was also a safety net—top-tier health insurance paid for all of my cancer care and surgeries and I never had to worry about going broke. I carried an incredible debt of gratitude, which kept me from exploring or making a career change. I stayed because it was easier than rearranging this part of myself.

We saw Dr. Barber again, before the surgery to remove the newest tumor. Thankfully, it was in a location that wouldn't be too complicated to excise. Her colleague, Dr. Humphreys, would be taking the lead this time. We were practiced at going to Seattle, for surgery and everything that entailed. The procedure, if all went to plan, might be outpatient, no overnight stay required. I was relieved at the prospect. I woke up feeling light and bright and I told the nurse no wheelchair was needed, I could walk to meet Lindsay with no trouble. He was incredulous for a moment and then agreed. He walked next to me, looking on in amazement. As we passed a nurses' station, he nodded to them, pointing at me and says:

"See, that's what clean living will get you, right there."

I chuckled. Dr. Humphreys and team informed us that the tumor had started to attach itself to the flap, the borrowed and rebuilt parts of my face. He'd been able to remove 98% of it, but there were remnants of tumor left behind, too challenging to extract without disrupting the reconstructed areas.

We were back in the cycle of recurrence and mitigation. There was no treatment. Surgery could help stave off further spread of the tumor but it would not prevent its return. Explaining this to people was a challenge, because our popular understanding of cancer is that you either have it or you don't, and if you don't, you must be fine, right? There's not much nuance in this view, so recurrent and untreatable cancers really mystify people. *No, I don't have cancer right now but I probably will again because it's aggressively recurrent and there is no treatment.*

I reasoned this disease would probably end my life—or become so intractable that surgery no longer made sense. No one could predict the timelines, but I figured the prospect of living to the average 4,000 weeks was unlikely. Maybe I would get to 2,800, age fifty, which would give me another ten solid years. The idea of living to this age, and living well, didn't bother me but I needed to pause, to zoom out and consider what I wanted, knowing that my journey with cancer was still unfolding. I decided to take a sabbatical and step away from work.

The idea felt audacious—being on leave for a long period of time, as long as I could manage, and then focusing my full attention on other pursuits, dedicating time without the demands of a forty-hour work week. This was going to be an experiment—I would improve my flying, dedicate serious time to writing and reflection, travel and see friends. I was going to read books and be outside and fly at Tiger Mountain whenever I could. I wanted to find ways to give back to the flying community I'd come to know and love, to help other pilots and support the school where I'd learned. I would spend more time in the sun, away from screens, and peer into who I was now.

I would use the time well and disconnect from working life, making space to sit and meditate, to better understand the past ten years. My thirties had been stable, but busy; we were always in motion, working on the house, building careers, driving to Seattle. The times of real rest were mostly under anesthesia, in hospital beds, or at home after surgery.

And even then, I was restless, eager to jump back in as soon as physically possible. I hadn't ever stopped to consider the totality of these experiences, how living with recurrent disease had shaped and changed me.

I felt guilty and undeserving at first. I wasn't sure I deserved to take a sabbatical, to go on an extended leave. My company had made many allowances over the years and perhaps I hadn't yet repaid the debt of gratitude. I knew my coworkers would get on just fine—they had before when I needed time to physically recover. But this was something different, I was going to put a pause on the whole notion of having a career. The people in my organization rallied around me. I was humbled, knowing I had support. I met with our CEO and talked about my intentions, how I would use the time, what I wanted to learn, the flying I would do.

"You know, hearing you share this with me—your story —I want you to know, I'm inspired. Truly."

Me? Inspiring? Very little about my life in that present moment felt exceptional or inspiring. Plus, attaching that word to myself, to my life, felt arrogant and contrived. I wasn't about to start proclaiming that I was a model for anyone. But perhaps there were parts of my story worth sharing, if for no other reason than to document them for friends, family, and the coworkers who encouraged me. I decided I would write during my time off, every day, and share my journey. I didn't know it then, but I would find healing in notebook pages, blog posts, and essays.

After the flap surgeries, I'd been terrified that a speech deficit would disrupt my ability to work. I'd been changed, my face refashioned, and the days of speaking easily, communicating with my mouth with little conscious effort, had come to an end. I'd returned to work after the surgeries and was able to get by, but the loss was noticeable—I noticed, even if other people said I sounded fine. Speaking would never be the same and moving through the anger and grief into acceptance had taken years. Eventually, I realized that I was not my voice and arrived at acceptance, just as I had with the realities of my cancer. And so I decided to write more, to channel ideas into another form, to practice and develop skill.

I started planning and created a set of goals for my time off, things I wanted to achieve. I was no longer guilty. I felt empowered, eager to dedicate myself to learning and being present. I made a diagram, a cancer roadmap, to tell the story of everything that happened, to remind myself, because all of the dates and events were beginning to blur. Ten years was a big deal—all of my thirties had been spent living with and living through cancer that couldn't be cured. We sure had tried, though. I was on the brink of turning forty years old and if I made it to fifty, that would be cause for celebration. Since all of this started, since the runny nose, the allergist, the diagnosis—I'd been sitting with the idea that I might not live to a ripe old age like my grandparents had. The prospect of dying felt like a fact, an eventuality, and maybe it would be sooner, because of the cancer.

Unlike the struggles with eating and speaking, the prospect of my own death didn't bother me. There was never a moment of anger or bargaining or dropping to my knees and screaming at the heavens. I accepted the randomness of the cancer, the awful timing, the potential I'd die this way, younger than others with more mainstream diseases. But ten years back, all those things were hazy abstractions. Now I had taken some real hits, I'd been damaged and changed and rebuilt—I had to accept and try to love a new self, one that was unfamiliar for a while. I'd become someone new, without really knowing it, beyond the reality of my physical limitations. I had a different sort of knowledge, born from experience, about what dying might actually look and feel like. It wasn't scary, it would be more like letting go, choosing not to cut away anything else because we'd already done enough. *I am going to die this way, probably.*

Saying these things out loud and plainly can upset people. People wanted to believe that a cure was possible, if not inevitable, that science or faith would deliver me from this outcome. Often, they hadn't considered their own end. The reality of your life, its brevity, is uncomfortable at first, seeing it clearly and knowing you cannot outrun it. I learned that sitting with this knowledge, accepting it, is freeing. I was straightforward with friends and family and coworkers—I have untreatable cancer that will probably, someday, end my life. Not today, but eventually. Maybe in five years, maybe ten. Either way, this was the reality and the reason for my sabbatical. Saying this didn't feel *inspiring*, it was just truthful. Sometimes people would thank me for being open about my life and share a personal story, an event they'd been through that brought them face to face with mortality. My understanding of what it meant to be helpful, through sharing and relating, was broadening.

I had half a year, a blank calendar of opportunity, enough time to imagine what retirement might be like. I shared the goals I'd set, which centered around progressing as a pilot, contributing to the flying community, traveling, and writing. I set another goal that was centered on my career—to try and find some clarity on what would come next, how I wanted to spend the rest of my working years, knowing I might only have another ten. How would I convince another company to hire me? Did I even know what I wanted?

The fact that I was taking this much time, that I'd allowed myself permission to stop working, surprised me. I needed a break from working life to refocus and understand the person I was now, after ten years on this journey. I was curious about what I'd learn with so much open space.

During my P2 training, when I was learning to fly, I'd heard mention of an event in Chelan, something related to paragliding that my instructors were involved in. I asked around and learned it was a competition. Having no real understanding of what a paragliding competition was, I told my friend Austin that I'd be willing to help—I had lots of availability. He smiled.

"I know exactly the job we'll give you, you're going to love it."

Chelan

I knew that my instructors and several other folks in the Tiger community would compete in paragliding events, but what these competitions involved was a total mystery. And the eastern part of my own state was also unfamiliar— beyond the day trip to Saddle Mountain, I'd never had a reason to traverse mountain passes and venture eastward.

Volunteer Coordinator was the role I'd assume for an event I barely understood. The not knowing was a challenge, which was part of the appeal. I would throw myself in completely because there were no other obligations or distractions. Work was absent from my mind, it had only taken a week or two to disconnect. This was exactly what I needed to be doing—helping, working in support of something I loved, flying and the community around it. Before my time in Chelan, the only paragliding competition I'd heard anything about was an event called the Red Bull X-Alps, a race that involves hiking and running and flying in the mountains. Lots of super fit European dudes competed —it looked like the paragliding equivalent of an Iron Man race, which is probably why I didn't give it much thought. Things that were 'extreme' and 'elite' didn't usually hold my attention. I didn't consider paragliding an extreme sport, certainly not the sort of flying I was doing. And if the barrier for entry was low enough so middle-aged folks with bad joints could learn, extreme wasn't the right word. The adrenaline seekers who buzzed treetops at 60-100 mph in wing suits and on speed wings were doing something extreme. Flying an entry level B glider in smooth conditions, by comparison, is pretty chill.

The format of the competitions in Chelan was a race, with a starting area and finish, and waypoints along the track. The main difference was the race took place in the sky and the competitors and scorekeepers used trackers and flight instruments. Each day, a committee of expert pilots and race officials would gather to set the task, which was highly weather dependent, as all things in paragliding are. The total distance, the goal, the waypoints and turns would all be set and mapped out, and then distributed electronically to everyone competing. The idea was to fly fast, but you also needed to stay in the air, using warm, rising thermals to maintain altitude. The pilots who flew fast through all of the way points, making it to goal, would be awarded points, which were tallied at the end of the week.

Orchestrating this sort of event with 120 competitors is involved. My job was to manage the operational aspects of the event—things that needed to happen in the background—so the meet director could focus on structuring an enjoyable and safe race. Things like work assignments and schedules, checklists and waivers, corralling people, helping aim their effort in a single direction. Wrangling kittens.

I didn't know any of this when I rolled into the volunteer

campsite, my Honda hatchback filled with camping gear and my blue and orange wing. I'd had a few calls with last year's volunteer coordinator, who briefed me on the high level responsibilities—making sure everyone knows what needs to be done, along with how and when to do it, basically. There was also a spreadsheet, which peaked my interest. I would need to do workforce management and assign tasks, rotating people in and out of jobs, which seemed simple enough. In addition, this group of people, most of whom were pilots, wanted to fly, which was one of the perks of volunteering. We'd need to find a balance between work and fun that kept people engaged and the competition well supported.

After the first day, I had a pretty good idea of the key activities, roles, and workload. Our morning briefings, just after breakfast, set the tempo for the day. There were daily raffles with hats and shirts from event sponsors, and then the chatter would quiet as Matty—the meet director— spoke, highlighting important developments, pausing every so often to smile and laugh.

"We had a great task yesterday and sixty pilots made it to goal, which is great. Thanks everyone for your hard work. Today we're expecting favorable weather conditions, probably a task out over the flats—so—remember to stop and get gas in your vans before heading out on retrieve. It's a remote area, no gas stations around, you wouldn't want to be stuck out there, low on fuel."

There was always a note, a reminder, a thing to emphasize, usually towards the end of his speech. I would speak next and welcome any new volunteers who'd arrived at camp, introducing them to our crew. A whiteboard was attached to the large oak tree we sat under, secured with rope and knots, the day's assignments listed out. Everyone had preferences on the jobs that needed doing. Some loved driving retrieve, picking up pilots who had sunk out and landed, while others preferred meal prep, staying close to camp and finishing the day's work earlier. I resolved to do each and every job myself so I understood what was required to do it well, so the team could see that I was committed, a working manager.

Not everyone was thrilled about working in the desert sun for free. Some of the jobs were unglamorous, but the potatoes needed peeling and dishes would have to be washed. I quickly learned who the all-star volunteers were, the folks willing to do any job I assigned, who beamed and bounced along, knowing there would be time for fun and flying later. I rewarded my best volunteers—they got to choose their favorite retrieve vans and I made sure they knew when flying opportunities were available.

Early risers usually had an opportunity to make asks before the day's plan was finalized. "Hey Jonathan—so I know you were thinking about putting me in a van today, but... " The outcome of this conversation, how willing I was to make a change, depended on my assessment of this volunteer, how much they'd been contributing, how long they were volunteering, how well they took instruction. In my mind, this wasn't playing favorites so much as giving incentives for hard work, and I'd make sure the give and take was clear.

"Okay, yeah that's fine. For tomorrow, I'd like to get you on retrieve—how's that sound?"

"You got it, boss."

A small few were the opposite of all-stars. They were complainers, people with too many reasons why they couldn't do this or that job. The goal, it seemed, was to do the minimum amount of work, while finding time to fly as much as possible. The disengaged few took more of my time than anyone else because I was constantly keeping them on task, giving them reminders when they should have taken initiative. They'd wander off, doing some random ass thing when a job needed to be done. Perhaps they hoped someone else would do it, someone more motivated.

"Where the fuck is Jason?"

We were on launch, and less than two hours ago I'd been very clear in our morning briefing about expectations— when we are up on the Butte and the launch window is open, you need to be helping the competitors, all hands on deck. I'd even come up with a little adage: everybody fluffs. But Jason was not fluffing—helping lay out wings, ensuring safe launches—he was off in the distance fiddling with his camera. I was enraged.

"Jason!" I yelled, loud as I could, which wouldn't register as yelling to most ears.

"I need you to go help on launch." He looked confused.

The distribution of work, the people who excelled, those who slacked, was plain for all to see. The majority of our volunteers understood that our primary purpose was to support the pilots competing and the team designing the competition's tasks each day. Flying was a nice perk, but it wasn't the main event. Every day was unique, but when tasks were happening and the weather was ripe, the structure was familiar and grounding. Breakfast, morning briefing, vans to pick up pilots, trucks to launch to set up. I was usually at launch before the competitors, unloading shade tents from a trailer, moving orange water dispensers onto folding tables. All of the day's jobs were assigned and people were in motion.

Scores of competitors arrive at the Butte and begin laying out gear, unfurling harnesses from compression bags, securing touch screen instruments to velcro cockpits. There are moments of waiting when all of the checklist items are complete and we are watching the competitors who are also waiting for the launch window to open. Usually, someone in our crew steps forward to serve as the 'wind dummy' and take a flight so everyone can see the emergent conditions in the air. Generally, we'd give this job to more experienced pilots, the ones who have flown in a variety of conditions and accumulated significant airtime. I am not a wind dummy because I'm too new and my role requires my attention here.

The race's start time is set, the pilots have been briefed on the task, and now everyone is in a scramble to launch. There are four launches to choose from, but trends quickly emerge and a queue forms. By now the sun is baking the cracked rock earth and our competitors are encased in elaborate pod harnesses, donning puffy coats and headgear—it's colder at 12,000 feet. We lay out wings with care and watch as a gaggle begins to form high above us, a wide circle of pilots flying red and orange and bright white wings with fillets of contrasting colors. They are climbing and circling and waiting until the race officially begins.

Our work changes once all of the competitors have safely launched. The meet director and safety coordinator commandeer a van that will act as a chase vehicle, monitoring progress in real-time, listening to the official radio channel. I've made the retrieve assignments for the day and my drivers are away, down the Butte and into the surrounding flatlands. A small team will provide detailed instructions to my drivers, watching on big screens, anticipating where people might land when sinking out, dispatching vans to fetch competitors. Everyone in the competition, and all of our vans, are outfitted with GPS trackers the size of a deck of cards and our retrieve dispatch team can see real time data on location, altitude, and more. Little glider icons dot the screen and twist around as pilots climb in therms and then break away from the cluster, moving forward along the sky-bound raceway. My phone is lighting up with back and forth between the dispatch team and the drivers. Often, the instructions involve driving until cell service can be found, near a pin-drop set of coordinates. I've tried to assign this job to people who enjoy thinking on their feet, who are decent at improvising. The dispatchers will tell me if a driver fails to follow instructions, which could mean a competitor out in the desert sun for longer than we want.

Driving retrieve is a highly variable, unpredictable assignment. You might end up in the open and desolated flatlands, driving around for hours or could be lucky enough to be in the van that's sent to goal, where everyone is celebrating a successful task. After all of our competitors, over 100 people, have been accounted for, the vans and drivers and GPS trackers all return to volunteer camp. By now, dinner prep is probably underway, with rows of onions or potatoes laid out, ready for chopping. I loved doing the prep work and often I'd enlist a few others to help. We'd make a game out of it, and see who could slice and dice their portion most efficiently.

The end of dinner sometimes presented an opportunity for flying. Sunset was late this time of year, 8:30-9ish, and so we'd take a van up to the Butte and fly to the soccer fields in smooth evening air. The barreling thermals the comp pilots had flown in, up to cloud base, were done for the day. From the sky we could see the low sun over the ridge, the Columbia River, and the winding steppes of Chelan Butte. These slow, calming flights were a welcome coda to the demands of the day, the heat and traffic of restless pilots. This incentive, our flying time, was a gift.

Summer in Chelan was hot and dry with dust devils and wind storms that might rip through without warning. New volunteers learned how to lay out wings on launch for competing pilots and everyone knew if they heard someone yell "dusty!" you needed to keep that wing on the ground at all costs. Kneel on the canopy, draping your body across it, but react quickly. You needed to make sure the miniature tornado could not catch the fabric, otherwise the pilot cold be plucked and tossed, helpless against a violent and powerful swirl of air. People had died this way here. Being focused and aware was paramount.

Volunteer camp, like any other place with people living in close proximity, had drama and conflict. I was rarely at the center, but I always heard about it because I was eager to listen. Our head chef would often find me and speak freely about whatever and whomever was top of mind, the people who weren't doing enough work, plates that had been left out which attracted bugs, the family with the ill-mannered teenager.

"Okay—so remember how I've been telling you about our friends over there, by Tyler and Sam? Well, they are doing it again, coming into camp, where we are living right now, our home, and making a giant mess and then just walking away. And who cleans it up?" She pointed both index fingers squarely at her chest.

"I do. I can't keep doing this. People need to clean up after themselves. We are all grown-ups here. Most of us anyways."

Meal times and cleanup duties were an ongoing source of stress and conflict. My years as a people manager had taught me the importance of listening non-judgmentally, allowing people the space to work through their emotions. I was damn good at it and I loved all the gossip and chatter. I needed to know what was going on and I didn't mind the extra details and colorful commentary.

We had a weather day during the competition, which meant the volunteers got a day off. I took acid around noon with five friends. We set out to the lake and our buddy offered to be our sober guide. We walked through a wooded trail that felt like a tunnel to an enchanted forest with sprites and fairies. The plants gave off a pristine and nurturing glow. Everything was brighter with a warm light and rounded corners. We talked about our lives and families, the hurts we carried, the ways we tried to love and accept ourselves. It was so easy to be honest because we were safe and together in this green place that was alive with sunlight.

I felt awash in a contentment that was similar to flying—unattached to any memory or want, any object beyond the present moment. I felt at peace with my body, like all of the tension—in my neck and jaw and shoulders—had been smoothed out, massaged away from the sunlight. The pain I'd endured, the moments of isolation, and the unknowns had brought me to this place in time. I was grateful for the difficulties because those experiences had given me so

much, more than they had taken away. My dreams, my
priorities, the people I cared about, the person I wanted to
be—all of it was in high contrast now, and there was an ease,
a knowing, that I would be okay, no matter what. I would be
held and cared for, supported, loved. My friends were here
with me and all of the kindness and gratitude took my
breath. We lay in the grass and saw clouds that were places
we could go, shapes that inspired and comforted us. We saw
people swimming in the lake and wondered what their lives
were like. They were so far away, as if we were 3,000′ above,
soaring beneath a banner of clouds.

We went back to camp and sat next to my tent, listening
to a song on headphones—*Only a Dream* by Camera
Obscura—a lilting ballad about lost love, heartache, and
finding strength to move on. The sharp edges of the ridges
that hemmed in our valley were glowing gently. I cried and
cried for the first time in years, grateful and overwhelmed
by the natural beauty and wistful lyrics. I took out my notebook and wrote for a while. I was learning so much just
sitting and listening, to truths I'd always known but now
had new words for.

Morning routines were like home, stretching, sitting
quietly to greet the sunrise. Volunteers rotated in and out
over the course of those weeks. My newest neighbor, also a
morning person, noticed my practice of meditative
stretching and asked me about it. We began to share coffee
every day, chatting as his dog bounced and darted around
camp. One morning he asked me something that catches me
off guard: *what advice would I give to my twenty-five-year-old
self?* I'm surprised, and then confused. Why is he asking me?
Am I qualified to give advice? My memory of twenty-five is
scattered but I know I had fun, that I was aloof, with few

expectations or plans for the future. I was happy and poor, independent and stubbornly opinionated. My face was less weathered, more symmetrical, before time and surgery. At twenty-five I was searching without awareness, trying on new selves, looking for one that fit. I told my new friend that a younger version of me, one his age, probably wouldn't take advice from an older man, that he would be skeptical and dismissive. He would not have possessed the maturity to seek out guidance, to ask a friend for help. My life now would be unimaginable to a twenty-five-year-old me.

I asked my younger friend about what prompted his question and why he believed I was equipped to answer and give advice. He explained that he was searching, and also struggling, figuring out what he wanted out of life, who he was. He understood that he was situated, as a young adult, in a place of change and transition; he was growing into and discovering himself. And so he figured that men who had lived through this stage in life would probably have something useful to say; he was asking what we would say to our younger selves, hoping to glean insight and wisdom.

I admired his thoughtfulness, his desire to learn. Maybe we saw in each other something familiar, separated by decades. I did not feel wiser, on the other side of my thirties, but I was not the same person. I hoped that I was kinder, more patient, with myself and others.

I'd been living in Washington for fifteen-some years but had never seen the desert east. I thought about all of the time I'd poured into my career, the house, all of those drives to Seattle for cancer-related appointments. There was still so much to see, so many places to fly, and now I was here, decoupled from the usual responsibilities, able to do something new and put my effort towards this improbable event

—a paragliding competition. I was so grateful I'd been asked to help.

The first competition came to a close and the participants celebrated with us at volunteer camp. Winners were announced, prizes were raffled. One of my instructors who'd competed encouraged me to consider signing up for next year's event. The idea sounded far-fetched. I was a new pilot, inexperienced and definitely not ready to do this sort of flying. Would I be having fun if I was in the sky for three, four, five hours at a time? How could I be comfortable in the air for that long? I was familiar with the techniques used to deal with peeing (diapers and pee tubes), but what about eating? Just getting through lunch was an ordeal, I had so many limitations that adapting to snacking in the sky felt like a tall order, something I'd need to have sorted well before I entertained the possibility of being in a competition. Plus, I still needed to build the bump tolerance and thermaling skills. Now that work was on pause, I would have some time to dedicate.

Higher profile pilots came out for the second competition. I was still volunteering, but handed over managerial responsibilities to Tyler the firefighter; I was too exhausted to run things for another week. On launch one morning, a tall fellow approached me, he seemed to know my name. He lifted the visor from his helmet—it was Nick, the very person who'd helped set all of this in motion, introducing me to my instructors, guiding me to Tiger and the community there. I thought about Katie and how she'd stayed in close contact, encouraging me to learn how to fly. All of this, the sabbatical, the competitions, the new friends I'd made and the flying—it was remarkable. I felt at home, in this place full of pilots. My lack of experience was met with thoughtful advice and guidance, I was welcomed, and little achievements were celebrated. We were all enthusiastic to simply fly in this place, awestruck by its vastness and rugged beauty.

I drove back home, over mountain passes, past bald ski resorts, through dense forests of evergreen. The skin on my face and hands had darkened several shades, tan and desert dry, lips chapped and wind broken. I was so fortunate—despite the cancer and everything that had changed in my body, I was alive and buoyant, able to fly and learn with other people who shared this same joy. I still had so much to learn. Maybe one day, some years from now, a competition might make sense. But for now, I needed to focus on the next steps, beyond the absolute basics I'd learned in my training. If I ever wanted to compete, I needed to become competent with XC flying, and to do that, I needed to learn the art of finding and then climbing in thermals. I was also approaching another threshold, where I would need to put my body, mind, and equipment to the test, and prepare for the unexpected, like I had seen at the competition.

Cross Country

The weeks in Chelan, living in a tent, waking up each morning to help others, broadened my perspectives on paragliding and working life. I understood the solo aspects of our flying were done best in the context of a community and now I'd seen what could happen when a big group focused their efforts and worked together. I was so proud of our volunteers and proud of myself, for leading them, not knowing anything about paragliding competitions and then immersing myself, becoming more than competent. I could imagine doing work like this, leading teams of people, running events, building towards outcomes that the organizers wanted.

Where my flying was concerned, I was no longer a brand new pilot, but I also wasn't quite at an intermediate level. There were skill gaps and I'd need to address before I could progress—learning how to handle potentially dangerous situations that might arise while flying, like a sudden collapse or concerning weather that might require a rapid descent. I would need the ability to react quickly, to understand what was happening without panic, without overreacting. If I wanted to fly in stronger conditions, I'd need to practice emergency maneuvers so I could guide my body and my wing safely through the sky. Before I progressed, and earned the next level badge, I'd need to do a safety course called an SIV.

I signed up for the clinic. The training course involves being towed up over a lake and then intentionally pushing your glider to the limit, with an instructor providing direction via radio. My name was last in the rotation, with more experienced pilots going first. I watched the sequence of events with the tows—the boat approaching the shore, the tow line being attached to the pilot's harness, and then the launch. In a few short minutes, at about 3,000', the tow line is released, and the high-intensity maneuvers begin.

Gaining altitude while tethered to a speeding boat is uncanny—your wing behaves differently, moves along unexpected axes, and requires unusual steering inputs. I watched a friend miscalculate just after starting his tow, landing in the water. The water, this whole lake, was our safety mat. Water landings were inconvenient, but rarely cause for alarm. We were all equipped with life jackets, and if one of our maneuvers got out of control and a reserve parachute needed to be thrown, we'd probably be shaken up emotionally, definitely wet, but uninjured. My launch and tow went fine and after a few minutes, I pulled the handle to release the tow line.

The first maneuver I needed to complete was a spin—a high G maneuver. I began applying brake, gingerly at first, and turning the glider to the left. I started to accelerate and heard my instructor: "More left brake, more left brake— more, more, more." Leaning hard, my left arm was extended straight down past my hip. The spin pushed me back into my harness and I felt intense pressure on my face, then sharp pain in my shoulder. I exited the spin and braced myself. *Oh shit, my shoulder is out.* I was repeating that first solo flight, when I'd briefly dislocated my shoulder, except now I was a few thousand feet up, over a lake.

Our radios are one-way and my instructor gave me notes on the first spin and told me to try again. I realized my left arm wasn't going to work until my shoulder was back in socket. Taking the steering controls in one hand, I raised my left arm in front of my body and straightened my elbow. I felt a familiar pop. I was pissed—it happened again. *Fucking shoulder.* There were no issues for eight months, and now this. I could feel this partial dislocation was more severe; my left arm did not want to move much, which was a problem, because I was flying. Maybe I was out of my depth, not yet ready for high-intensity training.

"If you can hear me take a left turn right now." I thought about ending the run and setting up to land. I gripped the brakes and made an easy left turn. I completed a few more maneuvers—inducing collapses and then watching my wing recover on its own. I set up for landing and struggled to flare, left arm pushing down hard on the controls, wincing in pain. I knew my weekend of training was over. There were more tows planned, another day of training, but I was done. I needed to rest and recover. Other pilots gathered around, offering encouragement and kudos. For the rest of the day, I watched from the beach, feeling deflated. I sat with feelings of self-doubt and disappointment for a while, but kept smiling. My shoulder recovered and I guarded it from certain motions in the air and on the ground and started doing physical therapy. The SIV experience unlocked something with the fear I'd been experiencing. I managed to work through a difficult outcome, one I didn't expect. My fear was there, but it didn't overwhelm me. I could see it, acknowledge it, and move forward. I made an assessment, calmed myself, and flew the glider. If I could stay safe with a dislocated shoulder, surely I could fly in active air and climb in thermals. And then maybe, with some practice and preparation, I could fly cross country. The pathway to doing this was starting to become clear. All I needed to do was learn some technique on finding and climbing in thermic air.

Since I'd learned to fly, I was traveling more. We went to Santa Barbara to visit friends and I flew at Ellings Park and a coastal site. I wanted to see more places, flying sites, and expand the range of conditions I could fly in. This was good practice and I trusted myself to stay within the margins of my skill. I wouldn't try to fly somewhere I wasn't qualified, unless an instructor was there to guide and observe. This was how people stayed safe, by taking small steps, progressing slowly. Slow was just fine, the whole point of flying wasn't to move at maximum speed, it was more about being in the air and seeing from a new place, moving gracefully through the sky, admiring the birds and mountains, the ocean and the forest. Flying was about the journey, the view—going fast was for speed wings and skydivers. I was more interested in flying up high and going somewhere, having the skill and tenacity to do that.

I enrolled in a clinic with a dozen other progressing pilots. I felt young in this group because most everyone else was fifty-plus, in various phases of being retired or nearly retired. Everyone was pleasant and curious, eager to build skills beyond the basics they'd learned in P2 training. We spent an afternoon kiting in the same field where I'd first learned how to inflate a wing. An instructor observed, offering advice on how to correctly control the glider. I didn't need much help because I'd been practicing and the foundational ground handling skills were a big part of my training, a prerequisite before I was allowed to fly. When I'd started training, a year ago, I imagined that in time my wing would begin to feel like my bike—sturdy, familiar, connected to me in such a way that I could sense and intuit what it was doing, like I could feel through it. And now I was beginning to have that same connection with this aircraft made of cloth.

Tiger was my home site and while I'd flown through some thermic air before, I didn't know what to do to actually climb, to gain altitude in a consistent way. I'd seen others do this at Tiger and at the comps, but that wasn't enough. There was something missing, a bit of technique I hadn't learned, an element I couldn't figure out on my own.

We were all here to learn this magic skill, how to find and climb in thermals. Our group gathered at Tiger's north launch and debriefed. The instructor spoke about thermal triggers, things to look for while flying that might be sources of lift—houses, barns with metal roofs, power lines. We knew how to fly, to launch and land, and now we would need to redirect some of our focus to finding lift. Our radios were set to a common channel, and as we explored our instructor provided a play-by-play. "It looks like Dan might have found something, he appears to be climbing, maybe fly over towards him." We were learning to be aware in a broader sense, watching other pilots and the environment for clues.

Turning in lift took practice and a coordinated set of

movements. The variometer, a flight instrument that indicates rates of ascent and descent with audible, pitched beeps, would start chirping when you entered a thermal. *Beep beep beep beep beep beep* faster and higher like a soprano singing scales. And then it would level off, or move in the opposite direction in sinking air. *Beeeeeeep* like a baritone holding a note, bending it down. This might tell you you'd flown out of the thermal. The trick was to fly straight into lift and keep that heading until it started to fit and then turn. If you repeated this sequences enough times, eventually, hopefully, you would find the center or core of the thermal. The rising warm air, being invisible, requires a different sort of attention, one that is unconventional and intuitive. We were running little experiments, trying to find lift that we couldn't see directly, observing how it acted on other pilots, on birds, making predictions about where the thermals might be.

With time and practice, and the company of other similarly skilled pilots, putting my wing into lift and making good use of it became easier, more of a game than a struggle. If I didn't find any thermals, that was fine, because I could always go land. And if I flew into strong lift, I'd be rocketed up, sometimes at a rate where my vario beeps started to blur together into a chorus. The more I flew in thermic conditions, the higher I wanted to go—I could get *above* the mountain I'd launched from, well above it, but still below where the airplanes flew. The altitude you might reach on a given day depended on weather and skill mostly, and on a good day at Tiger you might reach the top of lift and scrape the airspace—5,000 or 6,000 feet. In places like Chelan, pilots would reach double that altitude. Occasionally, when flying, we'd see a commercial aircraft in the distance, moving at speeds that felt unnatural. Birds flew at a more comfortable pace, especially when we would soar next to them, sharing the same thermal.

Gradually, I was able to consider more, to see and plan and act while also flying. An instructor once referred to this as bandwidth, the capacity you have to make decisions in the air. So much of this was mental, I was starting to understand that now. The competition-level pilots flew with an ease and grace that I envied—they had mastered something in their minds, through repetition and conditioning. I imagined their flying was meditative, calm and reflexive, like tai chi.

The months off, away from work but still busy learning, accelerated my progression. I flew with friends at beaches, over lakes, near the ocean, around the Butte. I could do more, little by little, with each flight, often trying something new—taking my hands off the controls at the top of lift, engaging my speedbar to travel more efficiently, landing where I'd launched from. I was becoming more comfortable in stronger conditions, more wind, bigger and punchier thermals. My launches were confident, well-timed; I knew exactly how much wind, even a whisper of a breeze, was needed to inflate my blue and orange wing.

I had it in my mind that my first XC flight would happen at Tiger, my flying home, the place I'd learned, where so many of my friends and instructors were based. There were a lot of considerations though. In order to fly out, away from Tiger and the familiar LZ, you needed the altitude to make it over the north ridge, at least 4,000'. Ok, I'd gotten up that high before, and soaring along the ridge, but I had never pushed past it. The idea of doing that, without a clear and certain landing area, seemed a bit insane. I needed to study a map first, and make notes, and probably also have a flight instrument with that map on it for reference. Or, I could try following a group of more experienced pilots, friends of mine, and they could help me over the radio if need be.

The flying season was winding down at Tiger by the time we tried, in late August. There was lift, but not enough to make it over the ridge, and the wind was moving in the wrong direction to travel very far. I was going to do a cross country flight soon, that was the next step, the next challenge, but it might not happen at Tiger this season. I was briefly disappointed but remembered the importance of patience and waiting.

I was not the same pilot after Chelan and the SIV. I had learned something about myself and built resilience. I was being mentored, finding inspiration and encouragement in the community of people who shared this improbable and beautiful thing. Every moment we spent in the sky was singular. I was present in a new way while flying, seeing the world from uncanny perspectives.

Returning

One of the goals I'd set was to figure out what would come next, after the sabbatical ended. There had been something brewing for a while with my job— a discontent and restlessness. These feelings sat in the background of my working life for three years, but cycles of cancer and surgery and recovery made it challenging to move on. I was tethered to the security of gold star insurance and the familiarity of coworkers who were friends, people who had supported me for many years. How I could leave? Wouldn't that be foolish, knowing the likely trajectory of my cancer? And didn't I still owe this organization something?

The idea of leaving was unsettling, so for a long while I did nothing. I stayed and tried to find new ways to grow, to create and contribute. I had been doing the same thing in the same place for nearly a decade and I wanted new challenges. I wanted the digital version of remodeling the bathroom. I wanted to be out of my element like in Chelan, because that's where learning happened. Doing something difficult, being immersed in the unknown, leading myself and others—this sort of work thrilled me. Maybe it was a talent—my enthusiasm and skill with messy problems that required unconventional collaboration, planning, and story-telling. I didn't know how to characterize these qualities into a job description—they seemed too broad, applicable to many situations and roles but altogether non-specific. I felt capable of meeting a new challenge, more confident now, but what did I want, exactly?

I wondered if I was too scattered, skills too disparate and hard to quantify, to find a new job. I'd managed to get some interviews before the sabbatical, with state agencies, for roles similar to the one I was in. I mirrored back what the panelists seemed to want, answering their multi-part, jargon-filled questions as best I could. But there were never any offers, just form letter thank yous. I tried to sidestep the disappointment, but I felt like I had failed.

I needed to do something new. Ten years was a long time to stay in one place. And it was impossible to disentangle my cancer from my career, and maybe that was part of the problem. I was good at planning, gifted even, but nothing about where I'd arrived in my career had been planned out. It had just materialized. Learning to fly had been an idea I held onto, a dream, something I envisioned and then finally did. My journey with work had been circuitous, unexpected, often chaotic.

During my time off, I'd decided that I would figure it out; during those six months I would force myself to have an epiphany and then finally know what was next. Maybe I'd even find another role, the ideal role, and go back to working life somewhere else. Learning how to fly, seeing the world while slightly removed from it, doing something wild and uncommon, had opened up my imagination. If I could summon the will to do this—to fly—maybe I was capable in other ways I hadn't considered. Maybe I needed to explore more, in my professional life, like I was doing in the sky.

I was lucky to have ended up where I did, with a career I hadn't planned for, and insurance that paid for the best care. I thought about an alternate reality where that didn't happen, where I'd stayed at the call center, fundraising to cover the cost of treatment, exhausting all of my resources to treat a rare disease. I was deeply grateful my career had unfolded in parallel with the cancer. I stayed because I was committed to the mission and happy to be alive and for a long time, that was more than enough. I survived cancer, and hostile managers, toxic coworkers, and then awful side effects of radiation. Helping others, solving problems, and doing work that was necessary and useful motivated and inspired me. And now, I wanted to do it somewhere else, in a different context.

But my plan had fallen flat—I didn't find clarity on what I wanted or where to go, there was no aha moment. I was still searching. I thought about the hospitals where I'd spent so much of my time, the experience of being a patient with rare cancer, navigating all of the messy choices and unknowns. My thirties had been shaped by the reality of cancer, almost like a part-time job, something I'd learned with no instructions. My providers guided and advised me, but there was a level of autonomy in the decision making, who I saw and when, how I used the information and knowledge. I'd heard and seen and lived through so many unusual experiences and now my life, as represented by a set of medical records, was quite exceptional. On the rare occasions when I saw general practitioners, they were often very alarmed after reading my chart, but also confused because I was never in distress; I spoke casually about the trauma of flap surgery and the intractable nature of my cancer.

I could think about it with a measure of objectivity because I had lived with it for so long. Cancer, for me, was routine. I wondered if this body of experience was something I could use to help others who were facing life-changing diagnoses. Maybe there was an opportunity to share the stories of others—patients and providers—to add depth to the idea of surviving cancer, to shine a light on the humanity and kindness of people like Dr. Barber and the surgeons she was training.

In the final months of my time away from work, I continued writing and flying, while also networking, meeting with like-minded career seekers. The ideal role was still fuzzy, shapes and outlines, like objects on the ground seen from altitude. I had so much more clarity on my flying. Next steps were obvious—continue practicing thermaling and then take a cross country flight, then another, longer one. Where my career was headed was unclear because I wanted to pivot into something new, where I would be a beginner, and maybe this was too ambitious. I had already taken an extended leave, progressed my flying, and built a consistent writing practice. Maybe that was enough.

Stepping away from work and finding purpose unattached to a paycheck reset me in ways I didn't expect. My understanding of career and its centrality in my life had guided most of my decisions. And now I was comfortable, having stumbled into the middle class. But the trade off was now clear. My time was not my own, not completely—a sizable part of it belonged to an organization. One that served the public good, but was self-interested, as all companies are. In the space of six months, with distance from work, I now understood the trade-off. I had done so much with my time away, and discovered a new sort of freedom, sitting with ideas and words, creating, developing a talent I'd only ever used in the context of my career, helping others by being available and present. I had so much capacity to give and to help when my calendar and my mind wasn't crowded out by the demands of emails and project boards. The constant din of IMs on a screen, the attention they required, had been reclaimed, and I could sit quietly and reflect, without all of the noise.

I became more appreciative towards myself in those months, kinder, less hurried. Maybe I'd been suffering from a version of what Hakan had described—a disappointment born out of constantly trying to do more, realizing the sum total of all the decisions you made as a younger person had not yielded the sort of life you'd imagined, that maybe you would make different decisions now, because you were not the same person. My friend and I traveled and searched, looking for meaning, trying to understand who we were and what we should do in life, where we should place our attention.

The time and energy you need for a cancer journey also requires new words, different ways of describing the enormity of its impact, one that is often permanent, if only on your view of self. I had trouble with the words 'cancer survivor,' as if I was placing a disease at the center of my identity. I didn't want to be anchored to a diagnosis, even as I was glad to affix my work, my appearance, and my abilities to this idea of self. I thought about this contradiction, because I had the space to.

There were moments of dread, or maybe disappointment, knowing I had to return. The likely reality of my cancer meant that retirement probably wasn't in the cards.

I worried that this preview might be it, that I would just continue working until I couldn't anymore, that I'd reach a point where the cancer would return, I would become terminally ill and then I'd skip the years of not working and go right into dying. It wasn't that the dying part concerned me; I was upset that the focus of my attention would be my career, that I might not have time to do much else.

Maybe there was such a thing as too much knowing, awareness that gives rise to some new discontent or skepticism, a seeing that can't be unseen. Lindsay reminded me to be grateful for the time I'd had, to have pride in what I accomplished. She liked the idea of me staying put, because we had stability there. But she also knew that I gravitated towards novelty and liked creating new challenges for myself, like I'd done with the bathroom remodel and planning the wedding. I liked the wide open possibility of doing something I'd never done before, learning in real time.

There were a few interviews, which I felt mildly confident about, but no offers materialized. I was not good at selling, and in general I was more interested in exploration, probing into new ideas and ways of doing things. I was not skilled at making a case for why a company should hire me, what value I would bring on day one. I was atypical. I did not check the right boxes to be the logical first choice for much of anything beyond the work I was already doing. And I'd spent so much time in one place, at one organization, that my ability to interview well—as a candidate—had atrophied. I wanted a change because my role felt too familiar. I needed to be doing something altogether new—a new company, new people, new goals. I needed something difficult, to be pushed; there was creative energy that had no outlet, which felt wasteful. I always felt like I could be doing more, even if people said I was doing enough.

I was disappointed there were no offers. I returned to my old job and was welcomed back with warmth. My colleagues had managed just fine, but they were pleased I'd be back, leading a team. The flying season was ending and my intermission from working life was over. I used the time well but the career change would need more consideration. I was just starting to understand what I wanted, hopeful it would lead somewhere, eventually. In the meantime, I would work and write and hopefully fly when the weather agreed.

My boss and close work friends knew I'd been looking elsewhere but the timing had been off and I didn't quite know where I wanted to go. I had the outlines, but they lacked the necessary detail. The first few weeks were confusing. I'd forgotten so many little pieces, acronyms, designs, and processes. The adjustment back to the chatter and endless notifications was painful. This had all been open space before, during my time away, like protected wetlands. And now it was being bulldozed. I was giving back pieces of my mind and attention that I had reclaimed, if briefly, and I could feel the loss in my eyes and energy. I wasn't going to have as much time outside because I would need to be stationed in front of a screen, responding in real time to one emergent issue after another.

Slowly, I adjusted and the hurried pace was my new normal. We moved through the week with a camaraderie and lightness that reminded me of my flying friends. It was good to be a part of a community, to contribute to something beyond ourselves. And that's what we were doing, even if the politics were fraught and conflicts ever-present, we supported and encouraged each other and made light of the absurd. I would miss this group of people if I left.

The fall season was damp and dark and flying was done for a while, which meant more reading. I started working in the living room, on my remote days, sitting on the couch next to tall stacks of books piled on every surface—the bookcase, coffee table, and the fireplace mantel. During my months off, I would sit in this spot and write, sometimes for an hour, sometimes four, depending on the day and my mood. Now, back at work, I relegated my writing time to an hour or so in the early morning.

My sabbatical was over which meant I was no longer documenting it for an online audience. I would need to pivot, like I wanted to do with my career. The goal of building a writing practice had been to hopefully turn it into something more substantial, to publish a longer form piece. I started experimenting, on the weekends, with concepts, ideas for essays, outlines of bigger narratives. I poured my soul into a few of them, essays that were wrenching to produce, but felt overwrought and bloated. I was missing some critical element, a binding concept that would hold the story together, giving it shape and texture, something you'd want to put your hands in. I kept writing different versions of the same thing, from slightly different perspectives, and the result was uninspiring, true but less than compelling.

I continued to read memoirs, books that were alive with detail, honest and memorable. Maybe I could develop that sort of skill, but probably not for a very long time. At least I had a benchmark, something to aspire to, like the goal of flying cross country. I'd seen friends do it, and I could too, someday. I knew what great looked like and could aim in that direction. I listened to authors and teachers talk about their books and the journeys to write them, the life they contained, the people they wrote for. I had my doubts I could actually write an essay, let alone a book. I didn't have the pedigree or the training—I'd never been a journalist or graduate student. I wasn't a qualified storyteller, just a person with an odd cancer story and paragliding hobby. How would I turn that into something people actually wanted to read?

I was back at my old job, finding contentment, and now I'd discovered an outlet, a way to channel ideas into tangible objects. I was energized and started to worry less about finding a new career. I wasn't sure how everything would coalesce, but flying was on my mind after months of being at home, writing in notebooks, peering into screens. I needed another break, a pause on the work, as much time as my meager bank of paid time off would allow. I decided I would go to Colombia.

Colombia

The people I knew who had dedicated their lives to paragliding—the ones who sold their houses to buy vans, left careers to become instructors—none of them stuck around for the wet fall and winter months in western Washington. There were a myriad of destinations around the world to choose from, where the weather was ideal for flying, where scores of other pilots would venture, for paragliding vacations or competitions. I knew people who went to India, Indonesia, South Africa, and Mexico during the off season, on tours with groups of other pilots (usually led by elite level instructors), or traveling there independently with no strict itinerary. I envied this sort of freedom, to travel and drop work for months each year, or altogether. I knew that Colombia was a popular paragliding destination and I'd heard stories of cross country flights my friends had taken there, with weather conditions ideal for thermal flying and soaring. I was going to find a way to get there, to fly in Colombia, and be in the sun for a while.

The last time I'd been overseas, or anywhere outside of

North America, was childhood. The army had taken us to
Frankfurt, Germany in 1985, early in my dad's career. I have
no memory of my time there, but there are pictures, and my
mom recalls that I loved the transatlantic plane rides.
Maybe my dream of flying had been imprinted early on.

If I was going to travel to a foreign country, to South
America, for the first time in my life, I needed company. I
floated the idea to Lindsay, but she was not interested in this
much adventure. Her preference was a sunny destination
that would involve more reading and less flying, Hawaii
perhaps. I reached out to flying friends, people with similar
experience, people I could imagine being next to in airports,
on planes, friends who had a low likelihood of travel-
induced grumpiness. I found a willing companion: Anton.
He'd been considering a trip to Colombia, but like me, was
wary of solo international travel. His wife, like Lindsay, was
adamantly uninterested. I offered to plan everything—
airfares, hotels, transport. We would sort out of the smaller
details when we arrived. Soon, tickets were booked, reserva-
tions confirmed, and our wings were folded and packed. We
were going to Colombia to fly.

I subscribed to an app and started learning Spanish,
using new vocabulary words and phrases alongside the
English equivalents. I studied up on the geography of the
area, the site we would be flying. Friends who were already
in Colombia gave me tips and WhatsApp contacts for bilin-
gual locals. I made at least three checklists and put my
clothing in compression bags. Anton reached out and asked
if his friend, a brand new pilot, could join us on the trip.

"Of course!"

We eased into full Spanish immersion, staying overnight
in Miami, near little Havana. The restaurant where we

ordered cervezas and chips with guac was playing telenov-
elas on flatscreens which were not quite level. The flight to
Cali was over water, mostly, shorter with better views than
the one from Seattle. Container ships dotted the seascape.
The water seemed motionless from 30,000'.

By the afternoon, we were in Cali, headed to Santa
Elena, a little town near the launch and landing areas
collectively known as Piedechinche, which literally means
foot bugs. I rode with Wilmar in a subcompact that would
only hold the two of us, along with all the luggage. My
companions were in another car that followed. Wilmar was
effusive and outgoing, he wanted to tell me about his life
and family, all of the places he'd traveled. He'd seen so
much of the world, competing internationally in basketball
with other wheelchair-bound competitors. I wondered if he
noticed that I moved differently, that I was thin in a way
people who'd undergone major surgery often are. Wilmar
pointed at things as we drove, saying the Spanish word,
waiting for me to repeat and then say it back in my language
—*rain, sugar cane, motorbike*. I thanked Wilmar for his
generosity and kindness as best I could. We had arrived at
our hotel, which was also a home and apartment building.
We dropped our bags and walked into town, quickly finding
a shaded spot to order cervezas and toast our arrival.
Tomorrow we would fly.

I didn't have a specific goal in mind—I knew that a cross
country flight was a possibility, but I wasn't going to push
myself after several months of not flying. I would ease back
into it, have a few simple runs where I flew right to the LZ,
so I would feel comfortable, familiar with the area from the
sky, before I ventured out. A friend I'd met in Chelan had
already briefed me on the key considerations: don't worry

about retrieve, someone will see you and give you a ride, try to land near a road if possible, be mindful of fences, power lines, and sugar cane. Simple enough. A half dozen of our friends had traveled separately from Washington. They could give me guidance, and maybe I would follow along on an XC excursion if the conditions were right.

The ride up to launch reminded me of Chelan Butte, except the dirt roads were dense, wet clay—there was no dust in this climate. We drove through tiny villages that looked like they were built into the mountainside. The air was dense—the opposite of Chelan, more like Olympia in the fall, but boiling hot at midday. Street dogs slept in roads, meandering slowly, unbothered by oncoming traffic. We bounced and jostled into each other as the 4Runner shifted into low gear, weaving around tight, uneven corners, over scars of washed-out red clay and rock beds. The trees were thick as the air, green and vibrant yellow. Unfamiliar tropical birds flew low and disappeared into the chirping forest. I felt elevated and giddy to be in a different country, heading to a new flying site.

We arrived at launch and unloaded our gear. The site was pristine and manicured, with a landscaper tending to decorative plants. The bare, grassy hill we'd launch from was wider than it was long, with a steep 20′ drop to the road below. We were surrounded by other pilots, carrying and unfurling gear, chatting and pointing at clouds. The town of Santa Elena was northwest a few miles, visible from launch as the clouds began to clear.

We were going to need to wait for a while because that was usually what happened. The ideal conditions might take an hour or two to materialize, and maybe they wouldn't at all. The predictive weather models we relied on in the US didn't exist here—we would need to wait and watch the sky. We took photos with friends and did preliminary gear checks. I ate some snacks and slurped down an electrolyte gel with caffeine. A channel of blue sky and sun had opened and the clouds were beginning to recede. This was a good sign, and pilots began moving with longer strides. There was less talking and more preparation. My friends were getting ready too, as lines began to form. Three gliders launched and then ten. We paid attention to the direction they were moving, their altitude relative to the launch. Soon, a sizable group formed a gaggle, circling in the same thermal, moving up towards cloud base.

I was ready to fly, nervous, but not more than usual. Even the comp pilots, ones with thousands of hours, seemed to have some form of this—the antsy, palm-sweaty feeling of anticipation, knowing you are about to fly. The motions replay in your mind, in sequence, inflating your glider, making sure everything is as it should be, airworthy, and then stepping away from the hill. My hands and arms knew where to be, how much pressure I needed to give to bring the glider overhead given the amount of wind, when to turn and then move forward. It all happened in seconds that felt like minutes because it was playing on repeat as you waited. I would always try to breathe deeply, to calm my mind even though my body was electrified.

Focused and quiet, in a single moment, my wing is overhead and I am flying away from the mountain. I glance up, pleased to see that nothing is twisted or askew. I checked before and during launch, but it's a good habit to look again. I know my wing will take care of and support me in the sky.

I am no longer nervous, ready to explore, to observe the pilots around me, to learn from them and the birds. The sky is full of other gliders but it's not crowded because the very nature of physical space is different here, more expansive than you would expect. I see the big gaggle that had started to form earlier and another, smaller group that's closer to me. I choose the easier option that also feels safer—the modest gaggle a few hundred feet away. We are circling round, pilots above and below, behind and out front. We are in a wide and generous thermal that is taking us all up at slightly different rates and I am focused and so thrilled that I could scream.

I continue climbing, in the company of other pilots and then a group of birds joins, blackish grey, with imposing wingspans, flying cautiously around us. I learned later they were Andean condors, some of the largest flying birds in the world. We are moving in concentric, drifting circles, going *up up up* but not straight up, more like a corkscrew held at an angle. The beeps of the vario start to sound lower and further apart so I fly in another direction, towards another thermal. Eventually, I am well above launch and the fields and roads below are missing details I could see before. There are several pilots, on red and white and orange wings who begin to move north, so I decide to follow. I am above them, and if I can stay that way, I should have no problem keeping up. The LZ is still reachable if I wanted to turn around. I know I could get there because I have a mental reference, having seen others land while circling overhead. So much of this flying and learning becomes intuitive, grounded in fact but based on feeling. I am only thinking about now, this moment, flying from where I am to another source of lift. I take a little sip of water from the tube on my shoulder. *Am I flying cross country right now?* I didn't plan for it to happen today, but the conditions were right, in the air and in my mind. I appreciate seeing other pilots nearby, people who have probably done this before, who can show me where the lift is. They are my weathervanes today, my mentors in the sky.

I've been flying for about an hour but it feels longer, there have been more decisions to make. I've been observing, seeing in a new way, paying attention to more than simply flying the glider. I suspect I've flown past Santa Elena but don't know for sure—I stowed my phone at launch because it overheated and shut off, so I am flying sans map. But that's just fine. I am confident I haven't flown very far, maybe a few miles at most. I see two, now three pilots who've lost altitude and seem to be setting up for landings in a nearby field. I decide to try to find just a bit more lift, I have time because I have altitude. I fly over farmland and dirt roads—there's some lift but not enough to get me back to where I was. It seems my cross country flight will be coming to an end. *Time to focus and find a safe place to land.* I've switched modes, having made this decision. I see two pilots on the ground packing up their wings in a dark brown field. I could go there but maybe it will be easier to get a ride if it's just me. I remember my friend from Chelan saying most of the retrieves will be on a motorbike as few people have cars here. I see a field that looks suitable, so I fly that way, making note of groundspeed and wind direction. I want to be close to the road, but not too close, because there are trees and fences. I land in grass and weeds that are taller than I'd expected, which isn't a problem. I'm reminded of the Tiger LZ, the reedy grass area we call the swamp, where new pilots often land after misjudging their approaches. Perfectly benign, but more work to get out of.

My wing is in a tangle of sharp weeds which sound like velcro as I peel them off the fabric. I am already sweating because it is hotter here on the ground than in the sky. I am surprised and proud and ready for a cold drink. My friends are still flying. I grab the radio and tell them I've landed out, safely. *My first cross country flight is in the bag.* A ride finds me as I pack up my gear—a young man named Luis. I hold tightly as we ride back towards town. I ask how much and he demurs, shaking his hand and head no. I insist and hand him a two mil bill. He didn't have to help me, but he did. I buy a large bottle of cold water from a corner store and walk back through town, down dirt roads, back to the hotel. I am exhausted and newly burnt from the equatorial sun. I want to tell everyone and celebrate my accomplishment. I've finally done it.

My friends were still flying, so I sat by the hotel pool, in the shade. I was surprised—I thought I would need more practice, more guidance, but maybe I'd simply needed to trust myself. Flying with company helped. I didn't know the pilots who'd been in the gaggle with me or the ones I'd flown with on my way north, past Santa Elena, but I was reassured by their presence. They were going out, away from the LZ, and I was keeping pace with them. I was starting to learn new ways of seeing, finding clues around me, little hints about where lift might be. And I was able to relax my brain and my body, so I could make decisions, without the fog of overwhelm. I was proud of myself. I hadn't planned a cross country flight, but it happened. I'd been encouraged—my friends, more experienced pilots, saw that I had the skills, that I just needed to try. I was grateful to have mentors, people I trusted, who were willing to help.

We hoped for perfect, consistent weather but the results were mixed—equal days of flying and not. Without forecasting, we made best guesses and decided whether or not to journey up to launch, not knowing the outcome. Rain was common, usually brief, which was not an issue most days. Prolonged storms could happen, which is why we watched the sky for signs, dark and foreboding clouds that lingered too long, growing in size, moving towards us—sure signs we wouldn't be flying.

On the fourth day of the trip, we'd already made it to launch as thick, tall clouds refused to clear. The likelihood of flying was more of a wish now. We had been waiting and waiting, hoping the sky would clear as it had the first day. But the conditions only worsened and the launch area became socked in by moisture. The temperature dropped and sprinkles became beads of rain, still intermittent but reason enough to grab your gear and move under a structure with a roof. The beads turned into sheets and a crowd of pilots—maybe thirty or forty—began gathering near the parked trucks, climbing in, lifting wings overhead. The rain was taking a pause but a storm was coming, judging by the frenzy. My friends jumped in the back of the last truck and pressed in close to other pilots. They had no desire to be here for a storm. There was no remaining space, so I wished them farewell and glanced at the handful of other people around me. *We are about to be stranded.*

Thankfully, there were hammocks. A gravel pathway wound up a little slope overlooking the launch, to a metal roofed hut made of thick bamboo. A row of fabric hammocks were tethered to eye hooks in zigzag pattern. I climbed into one, between a bearded fellow and a restless Southerner. The rain had started, blanketing everything. We were in a thunderstorm, and we would probably be there for a while. I wrapped the hammock around me, building a little cocoon. Thunder cracked as storm clouds surrounded us. We were in a storm, literally in it, at nearly 6,000'. Rain pelted the roof, running down makeshift gutters into gravel troughs next to flower beds. I was a little cold but dry, feeling lucky to be here, witnessing a storm in a hammock, on a mountain. I wasn't worried about finding a way back down, about being stuck. The other day I had flown beneath clouds and now I was sitting in them. *What a perfect way to spend an afternoon.* I closed my eyes and rested as the rain swelled and then lulled and then repeated its cadence.

The couple sitting next to me seemed restless, maybe annoyed, as did the British guys—a group of three we'd met at a neighborhood bar near the hotel. I introduced myself to the bearded guy. He also seemed amused at the situation we'd found ourselves in. My bearded friend was from Colorado, a relatively new pilot, on his first trip to Colombia. We laughed as the other people stuck here with us became more impatient, fumbling with phones, complaining about the unfairness of it all. I remembered something I'd learned in Chelan, during our time at the lake, about seeing the allure of convenience and not becoming too attached to it. Being here, stuck on launch in a thunderstorm was not convenient, but if you fixated on that, how could you enjoy the rain? Thunderstorms were so rare back home, in Olympia. This was a gift.

I thought about what it meant to be patient, how I was

still learning, how flying was giving me new opportunities to practice. I'd been impatient in my journey with cancer, in those early years—with the disease, with myself—unwilling to pause and recover, to slow down and grieve. I wanted to be in continual motion, and maybe that was a form of distraction. I was now in a state of remission with the cancer, but prepared for its likely return in the future. But I didn't need to worry about that now, I could simply sit in awe, in the present, here in my hammock.

After a while the rain stopped and the sky cleared. We found rides back down the mountain to the open-air cantina next to the LZ.

On our final day, before traveling back, we decided to venture to another location to fly. A local instructor named Juan Fernando would be our driver and guide. We loaded up our gear and headed northwest, into the mountains, towards Calima Lake. As we drove across the valley, Juan Fernando pointed out notable places, telling us facts. Buga, due north of Santa Elena, is known for a savory soup with beans and chicken, and people travel there to eat it. Jimbo, a friend of our guide, sits up front and as we accelerate up the mountain pass, tells us how he is certain— totally convinced—that aliens seeded the planet with life. And maybe they are still here, in the ocean. Anton and I glance at each other knowingly and smile.

After a brief stop to switch vehicles and pick up more pilots and gear, we begin the all-terrain drive up the mountain that lingers outside of Darien, the lakeside town. The road is more primitive than the one to Piedechinche and we slide and skid but stay on drivable surface. It's rained recently and there is brown-red mud and rainforest all around. We pass houses and farms, fields with cows and horses. The truck slows and stops ascending as we arrive at a property with several newly constructed guesthouses, and a view of the town and lake. The launch area is sloped, with ample space to lay out your wing and make a tidy reverse launch. The wind is sedate and the cloud is lower than we'd like, which means more waiting.

We drink coffee and eat snacks and pet the horses that peer at us from behind the wire fence. The clouds are moving now and the wind is gaining strength. Jimbo lays out a glider and inflates it overhead, unhooked from a harness, risers in hand. He's checking the lines for twists and knots. Anton's friend, the newest pilot in our group, is visibly nervous; he has minimal experience launching in higher wind, which requires well-developed kiting skills, which he also doesn't have. Several of the pilots we rode up with are laid out and ready to fly, then quickly away. I've checked my gear, readied my flight instrument. Anton launches and climbs up, flying down the ridgeline and then back again towards launch. I quickly prepare my wing, breathe in, and then pull gently, using the wind and my body to inflate it. I turn and bring my arms back as I prepare to move forward, towards the launch's end and then the wind filling my glider is gone, switching direction. The entire right half collapses like crumpled paper. I turn around quickly and gather the lines and fabric of the wing. This is why we make sure the glider is stable before committing to a launch. On a second attempt I'm in the air in a swift, controlled motion, flying, going up but not too quickly.

The clouds behind are darker, I can see more of them from up here. I begin to feel small droplets dotting my sunglasses. I use my foot to engage the speedbar and fly faster, away from the clouds and rain, towards the clear sky. I follow some birds and try to copy their movements in compact thermals. I manage to gain some altitude but not much.

The wind has picked up and I begin to worry about our new pilot friend. The conditions are now marginal, ill-suited for a beginner, and not exactly fun for me either, but manageable. As a newbie, a fresh P2, I wouldn't have launched. But if I had found myself in similar conditions, I would've been in full panic mode, unsure of what to do, unable to formulate a plan.

The wind is now tearing apart any thermal lift I find, blowing the warm columns of air into fragments, scattering them around. My wing tip takes a small collapse and immediately recovers. I see it and hear it—*thhhwack*—as the fabric snaps back like a wet towel. I knew I was going to land soon, and the landing field near the road into Darien—our original plan—wasn't going to happen. Below, in a pasture, I see two of the pilots who'd launched before me. I turn and then again and set up for landing, into the wind, which is stronger still. I am on the ground, right where I wanted to be.

Our guide was en route to retrieve me and two guys I'd landed with, as we made our way to the closest road. I wasn't sure where Anton was, but I trusted him to make good decisions. I worried about our new pilot friend—he was not equipped for these conditions, but was unwilling to admit it. The pilots, locals, speak to an older man on the adjacent property. There are several dogs they are concerned about, near the house, and they want assurances before we cross the threshold. I vaguely understand what is being communicated, mostly through their body language. The dogs are curious, but not aggressive.

We head into town and eat lunch at a local spot Juan Fernando likes. There's a lot of meat, but also a savory soup with beans that I can eat easily. Our new pilot friend narrowly missed an injury, which he's captured on his GoPro. He nearly made the landing area, but the conditions shifted. Knowing how to react, to safely improvise, requires experience, but he barely knows how to land. He'd bounced off of a barbed wire fence, but managed to avoid injury. I am aghast because he seems to find this amusing. I'm not his instructor but I know mine would be gravely disappointed. I wanted him to know his behavior was alarming, the sort of carelessness that could make you a pariah in the community. The people who had been flying for many years, the ones who were well-respected, avoided negligent types who were one bad decision away from a serious incident.

We return to a villa with a pool, where we'd stopped earlier to grab gear and other pilots. I find a hammock and rest for a while, tired from flying in challenging conditions. I am glad we came here, I am learning and pushing myself but this sort of flying is not a vacation. I was thankful the new pilot was unharmed and I want him to know that he should be more mindful. I remember the feeling of being new and not knowing, looking to others for guidance, imagining the voices of my instructors, their judgment. I committed to a slow progression and it's served me well; I was never going to keep up with those young guys, the naturally skilled ones. Finally flying, after everything else, is enough. I feel deep gratitude for the country I'm visiting, the people I am with, and the fact that we are here together, to fly. The hammock sways gently as I close my eyes.

Juan Fernando mentioned a ridge soaring site not many people know about, on the west side of the lake. We pack up and head there, parking along the side of the narrow, winding highway. The gate was supposed to be unlocked, but it's not, so we toss our gliders over and duck under barbed wire. Just over the little ridge is a series of pastures punctuated with fences along a gentle sloping hill, with the lake below. Ridge soaring in higher wind requires exceptional wing handling skill, which I am still developing. I had gotten to competence but was not yet to mastery. We arrived at the top of the slope as other pilots in our group readied their wings and harnesses. I told the skydiver that these conditions were beyond his skill level, and advised him to observe.

I launch into the lift band in the center of the bowl where two slopes meet and the wind takes hold and starts pushing me backwards, slowly. In Miami, we'd seen seagulls flying, in a stationary sort of way, letting strong wind hold them in place, hovering. I hear Juan Fernando yell "Speed-bar! Speedbar!" and I push it, and start moving forward slowly, into the wind and then across it. The lift band around our little hill is more gracious than the bowl I launched in and I soared without instruments, using my eyes to judge distance and altitude. Anton soon joins me and we fly close to each other and then away, back and forth along and above the lakeside hill. I remember skydiving— falling, then flying—viewing the world from a different angle, feeling captured by the moment, fully detached from other concerns. And now I was here, in the sky, with my friend. My mind is still even as my body and glider are moving through the air, soaring.

The wind began to pick up and I decided the afternoon soaring session, our last time flying in Colombia, was over. I made a few passes over the backside of the hill, losing more altitude each time, applying more brake, and then top landed—not elegantly, but well enough. With our wings packed we headed through pastures and grassy hills, down the mountain, into the valley, and back to the town of Santa Elena.

Juan Fernando drove us to the airport in Cali the next day and talked about learning and humility, how every flight has something to teach you, if you remain open. We boarded the plane and settled in, and I thought about what I'd learned in Colombia, the ways I was more confident, but still cautious, aware of my limitations. I hadn't planned a cross country flight, but it happened, I was ready and I flew further than before and landed safely. I celebrated with friends, proud that I'd passed this threshold, knowing how much work and thought it required.

My dreams of flying had taken me far from Tiger, to South America, and now I was on my way home. I was grateful, for the views from the sky, for friends to fly with and learn from. The disease and damage and surgery had shifted something. I was more thankful, for life and the people who I shared it with, the time I had, no matter how long. It was still cold in Washington but spring was close and soon another flying season would begin.

Acknowledgments

Brian Kennedy was the first person to hear me describe my early experiences with cancer and say: "I think you have a book there." I filed that away for years, but it never left my mind.

This book, and my writing, have benefited from the wisdom and insight of my editor Bailey Lang. It's been a pleasure to be your student.

Like Tiger Mountain, the University of Washington Medical Center at Montlake is a familiar place, with exceptional providers who have cared for me over the years. Dr. Brittany Barber, in particular, has shaped my understanding of what compassion looks like in the context of surgery and medicine. I'm in awe of the work she does and the way she does it. Tuyet Nguyen and Jamel Hicks: thank you for being so warm and welcoming in clinic.

Special thanks to Dr. Alan Sutton in the UW Dental maxillofacial prosthodontics clinic for building me a new smile. People sometimes ask if the wire around my front tooth is jewelry from a mouth piercing, which always gives me a chuckle.

My instructors at Northwest Paragliding have offered encouragement and support for this project ever since they caught wind of it; Austin Cox and Matty Senior—thank you —along with Luc Lachappelle, Robert Fitzgerald, Steve Forslund, and Forest Cox. It's a joy to fly with and learn from instructors and mentors who are now dear friends. Flying tandem with more experienced pilots helped my progression—Seth Brothers and Nat Mote, thanks for the sky coaching.

Hakan Akkan and Desmond Mills are two of my favorite people to be around in the sky or anywhere else—thank you both for eagerly reading advances and offering feedback.

Bronson McKinley graciously offered to lend his voice to the audio version of this book and it's wild how close his narrator is to the voice I hear inside my head while editing and revising.

Katie Schou at Send It Foundation has been part of this story since the early chapters—thank you for being an advocate for me and so many others in the YA cancer community.

My readers on Substack, many of whom are colleagues, friends, and family members: your continued interest and engagement has been important to my growth as a writer, and this book would not have happened without you.

My brother, Dr. Timothy Hutton, is one of my closest friends. He's been a sounding board for everything cancer related since the very start, and is a champion of my writing, sitting with early drafts and manuscripts, providing input on medical terminology, pace, and style.

Lindsay wanted to make sure I acknowledged Mabel, our sweet Great Pyrenees mix. She's kept me company on the couch during long writing sessions and her presence is a source of joy. To my wife Lindsay: thank you for listening to me ideate out loud, for reading drafts, and tolerating my single-mindedness. I'm glad to be writing and living these stories, with you.

Noteworthy Organizations

Northwest Paragliding
The Seattle area's only USPHA certified paragliding school.
Learn how to fly with a team of world-class instructors.
Tandem flights available and no prior experience is
required. Come soar with us: www.nwparagliding.school.

Send It Foundation
Providing young adults affected by cancer with outdoor
adventure opportunities and community. Find out more at
www.senditfoundation.org.

Head & Neck Cancer Alliance
Dedicated to supporting individuals impacted by head and
neck cancer, this organization is an important voice in
raising awareness and advocating for improved patient
outcomes. Learn more at www.headandneck.org.

About the Author

Jonathan A. Hutton is a writer, public servant, and ambassador for the Head & Neck Cancer Alliance. He can be found flying at Tiger Mountain, near Seattle, and resides in Olympia with his wife Lindsay and their dog, Mabel. This is his first book.

Follow him online at www.unflappable.blog